ATRIA BOOKS

Walking along the beach a few years ago, Helen told me her plans to write about Faith and Feminism. I told her that she must. Feminists must deal with the metaphysical. In her new book, Helen points us in that direction. This book is told from a Christian perspective, but the message is universal and compelling.

> —**Betty Friedan**, author of *The Feminine Mystique* and founder of N.O.W.

Feminism today must reclaim the power and truth of religion, which have historically grounded women's commitments to justice and wholeness. Helen LaKelly Hunt offers us a powerful guide for doing so. She shows us how to live with courage, integrity, and love.

> —**Rita Nakashima Brock**, former director of Radcliffe College's Bunting Institute and leading scholar in women's studies and feminist theology

The Jewish concept of *tikkun olam*—repair of the world—is given rich human expression in the commitments and accomplishments of the five Christian women profiled in this inspiring book. Helen LaKelly Hunt unmasks the false dichotomy between faith and feminism and challenges us to embrace synthesis, inter-connectedness, and activism in pursuit of justice.

> —**Letty Cottin Pogrebin**, founding editor of *Ms.* magazine and author of *Deborah, Golda, and Me: Being Female and Jewish in America*

Faith and Feminism reminds us that the promise of the feminist revolution is nothing less than transformative. It frees us from the narrow definition of religion, place, gender, and class and enables us to embrace a wider and deeper sense of being connected with one another and the world.

—**Kavita Nandini Ramdas**, President
and CEO of Global Fund for Women

Groundbreaking! A woman who understands the deep significance of life. Helen LaKelly Hunt shows us the rich significance of the American women's movement's roots in the Christian faith tradition. Pointing a way to bridge the bitter divisions between women of faith in the U.S. and feminists, Hunt takes us back to the "cause of God" of the nineteenth century, the abolition of slavery. In 1837, white and African-American women banded together to hold the first national political women's meeting to "unite heaven and earth" and to transform American society by daring to live the democratic and religious ideals America has always espoused. Using stories of nineteenth-century firebrand and Quaker minister, Lucretia Mott; Sojourner Truth, the powerful orator, leader of the Underground Railroad and former slave; St. Teresa of Ávila, the first woman Doctor of the Church; contemporary Catholic activist, Dorothy Day; and the New England poet, Emily Dickinson, Hunt inspires us with every anecdote. By example, she invites women of all spiritual traditions to unearth the feminists inside their faith.

Hunt does us all enormous service with this book by delineating the biggest obstacle to social change today—the division between women of faith and women of action. Then she goes further, showing us in her unique way how transformation emerges naturally if we will only listen to the words of these narratives. Change arises from the interior, and we are led to loving action by the divine. Faith and feminism cannot *only* co-exist today but they need each other tremendously.

>   —**China Galland**, author of *Longing for Darkness: Tara and the Black Madonna* and *The Bond Between Women: A Journey to Fierce Compassion*

At last, Helen LaKelly Hunt has given us a book that candidly and helpfully addresses the troublesome divisions between feminism and faith. Using the engaging stories of five courageous women along with her own powerful story as a feminist and woman of faith, Helen makes a strong case for the necessity and the possibility of healing this damaging split. *Faith and Feminism* is a must-read for all feminists and for all women of faith. I guarantee it will give us hope that our lives, our societies, and our world can be transformed.

>   —**Joy Carol**, author of *Journeys of Courage* and *Towers of Hope*

FAITH
AND
FEMINISM

 A HOLY ALLIANCE

Helen LaKelly Hunt, Ph.D.

ATRIA BOOKS

New York London Toronto Sydney

ATRIA BOOKS
1230 Avenue of the Americas
New York, NY 10020

"Sunday School Circa 1950" from *Revolutionary Petunias & Other Poems*,
copyright © 1970 and renewed 1998 by Alice Walker.
Reprinted by permission of Harcourt, Inc.

Picture Credits: Emily Dickinson courtesy of Amherst College Archives and
Special Collections; St. Teresa of Ávila courtesy of Friar Robert Lentz, O.F.M.;
Sojourner Truth courtesy of National Portrait Gallery, Smithsonian Institution;
Lucretia Mott courtesy of National Portrait Gallery, Smithsonian Institution;
Dorothy Day courtesy of Marquette University.

Library of Congress Cataloging-in-Publication Data
Hunt, Helen LaKelly.
Faith and feminism : a holy alliance / Helen LaKelly Hunt.
—1st Atria Books pbk. ed.
p.   cm.
Includes bibliographical references.
1. Christian women—Biography.   2. Feminism—Religious aspects.   I. Title.
BR1713.H79 2004
270'.092'2—dc22
[B]   2004050189
ISBN: 978-0-7434-8372-8

First Atria Books trade paperback edition June 2004

1   3   5   7   9   10   8   6   4   2

Book design by Ellen R. Sasahara

ATRIA BOOKS is a trademark of Simon & Schuster, Inc.
For information regarding special discounts for bulk purchases,
please contact Simon & Schuster Sales at
1-800-456-6798 or business@simonandschuster.com
Manufactured in the United States of America

ACKNOWLEDGMENTS

O ur *relatedness* to one another is inherent in our understanding of religion. The word "religion" comes from
the Latin word *religare* meaning "to tie back together, to re-
unite." It feels fitting then to pause, tie back together, and acknowledge the many relationships that have made this book
possible.

First and foremost, I want to acknowledge the five holy
women of this book—Emily Dickinson, Teresa of Ávila, Sojourner Truth, Lucretia Mott, and Dorothy Day. They inspire
me in my waking state, visit me in my dreams, and continue
to teach me through their honest and faithful lives.

Three women deserve special mention for their help with
the manuscript: Elizabeth McLaughlin, Jean Staeheli, and, at
the final hour, Sunita Mehta. For contributing research, foot-
notes, and overall care: Sally Lindsey, Susan Tive, Rachel
Provencher, Nedra Adams, Anne Morris, Bernadette Galle-
gos, Agapita Martinez, Elizaida Martinez, and Marcia Franco.
As we worked together, each of these women seemed to fall
in love with the five holy women as much as I had.

I thank Gloria Steinem for her loving influence and for
her role in catalyzing the second wave of feminism. This social movement has improved the lives of every man and
woman I know. In 1992, she reminded us that in addition to
the needed social revolution, there is a *Revolution from Within*

that women must address. Because I feel that the spirit of God is essential to this revolution, my conversations with Gloria on this topic are always provocative and enriching.

Now that I have completed this book on five historical women, I wish I had time to start another. It would be about five modern-day women: Tracy Gary, Marie Wilson, Idelisse Malave, Letty Cottin Pogrebin, and Christine Grumm, women who have dedicated their lives to empowering other women, uniting their faith with their feminism. I would add a sixth woman—Kanyere Eaton. As head of The Sister Fund, she and I support one another with many tasks—including our writing projects. But most important, she embodies, more than anyone I know, a deep wedding of her faith with her commitment to social justice. These six women share my interest in a radical faith that speaks to social issues, and they struggle with the conundrum of how women's spirits can flourish within patriarchal ecclesiastical structures.

I also thank Drs. Rosemary Keller, Delores Williams, and Janet Walton for their encouragement of my work at Union Theological Seminary. They embody the seamless interweaving of faith with feminist and womanist ethics. The writing and support of China Galland and Joy Carol helped me deepen my engagement with this material. I also want to thank Stephan Rechtschaffen for the opportunity to work on this material in workshop form at the Omega Institute.

I am grateful for Barney Karpfinger, my agent, who bravely took on this book and found such a fine publisher. I thank my editor, Brenda Copeland, for believing in this book, and for her unwavering enthusiasm. She and Tracy Behar have midwifed this manuscript into its final form.

Audre Lorde once wrote, "My silences have not protected

Acknowledgments

me. Your silences will not protect you . . . for it is not difference which immobilizes us but silence. There are so many silences to be broken." As someone who struggled for years to tell my own story, I acknowledge the role of trusting relationships, beginning with my friends Linda Tarry-Chard, Sara Waterbury, Carol Angermeir, Susan Bagwell, Janie McNairy, and Diane Garvin. We have shared so many of life's passages that we have become living diaries to one another. I also thank the spirited Imago Community for their consistent modeling of dialogue, empathy, and love.

I am ever inspired by my dynamic sisters Swanee and June, pioneers in their respective fields. I have a brother considered a feminist by Dallas standards. Ray is amazing, and I love him for many reasons, especially for bringing Nancy Ann into our family. I acknowledge with special gratitude my never-to-be-predicted husband, Harville, and his undying support of this work and of me. I am both blessed and edified by our six children: Josh, Mara, Kathryn (and her husband, Ron), Kimberly, Leah, and Hunter. Throughout the years, we have been teachers to one another—a gift so few receive and one I truly appreciate. In many ways, this book is dedicated to Jacob and Mary, my grandchildren, in hopes they will grow up in a society with more faith institutions of integrity and a feminist agenda that has succeeded in lifting all voices.

Everyone I have acknowledged has helped me in some way to better reflect on the stories of this book's five holy women, to articulate the messages they bring to us today, and to tell my own story. Life challenges each of us to find those who will help us break our silence, find our voice, and speak our truth. I challenge you, the reader, to find the people in your life who can support you with the unfolding of your own journey.

In 1859, Phoebe Palmer, a Methodist preacher wrote,

"The Church in many places is a sort of potters field where the gifts of many women, as so many strangers, are buried."

With the union of our faith and feminism, these buried gifts can be lifted up from the dust and received in the world with the dignity they deserve.
This book is dedicated to all those who cannot yet freely express themselves or whose gifts are yet to be acknowledged.

CONTENTS

Introduction by Gloria Steinem   xv
Letter to the Reader   xxi

Chapter 1   To Build a Dialogue   1
Chapter 2   The Journey Toward Wholeness   17
Chapter 3   EMILY DICKINSON: Claiming Your Pain   29
(1830–1886)
Chapter 4   TERESA OF ÁVILA: Integrating Your Shadow   41
(1515–1582)
Chapter 5   SOJOURNER TRUTH: Finding Your Voice   55
(1797–1883)
Chapter 6   LUCRETIA MOTT: Taking Action   69
(1793–1880)
Chapter 7   DOROTHY DAY: Living Communion   87
(1897–1980)
Chapter 8   Weaving a Connection   101

Afterword: Toward a Whole Feminism   119
Continuing Reflection and Dialogue   143
Appendix A: Resource Guide   163
Appendix B: Timeline   169
Notes   173
Recommended Reading   195
Index   201

INTRODUCTION

by Gloria Steinem

W*e're sitting* on an old and comfortable couch in my living room, talking about a book that Helen has just finished, the one you now hold in your hands. For more than thirty years, I've known Helen as a friend and colleague whose unique blend of faith and activism, gentleness and strength, are a kind of sun under which other people blossom. She has generously asked me to write the introduction, but I'm not at all sure that I'm the right person for the women of faith she wants to reach.

Yes, I share Helen's belief that women's spirituality has been and continues to be one of the wellsprings of feminism. This deep belief in universality has been expressed far outside the many patriarchies that make up organized religion, and also as a force for reform and meta-democracy within them.

But Helen is writing as a Christian with the courage and belief to reform the institutional Christian faith in which she was raised. By extension, her work applies to all the women and men who are striving within their traditions of Protestantism or Judaism, Catholicism or Islam, to, as she writes, "encourage religious women and men to consider feminism as an essential in the divine plan for love and justice." It also applies to women like me who find spirituality outside religion, and it will serve the second of Helen's purposes—"to help secular feminists begin to trust the possibility that faith can lead people to effective activism."

Still, why should believers in a church or mosque or temple listen to me? I am not a Christian. I am not even a monotheist. As the child of a father born to an upper middle class Jewish family and of a mother from a working class Protestant one—a marriage considered "mixed" in their generation and opposed by both families—I learned early to question any religion that claimed to know the superior way.

Growing up, I mostly absorbed the teachings of Theosophy, a blend of science, mysticism, and spirituality that had attracted and held my mother and both my grandmothers by the time I was born. It had an appeal for me, too.

Sitting with my coloring book in the back of Theosophical Lodge meetings, I sensed the respect with which children were treated, perhaps because the Theosophical belief in reincarnation countered any idea of children as possessions, or blank slates on which parents could write anything. I also loved the idea that all living things were linked rather than ranked, especially given my identification with animals. In retrospect, I probably benefited from seeing women's leadership in Theosophy. Many years later, I learned that such suffragists as Annie Besant had been drawn to Theosophy, perhaps because the rough justice of reincarnation allowed them to imagine cruel patriarchs being re-born as women.

But none of this equipped me as an adult for anything more (or less) than a respect for teachers like Jesus (who countered the hierarchy of his day by "caring for the least of these"), or Mohammed (who was an important reformer for women's rights in his time), or for such Jewish rituals as the

Seder (a ceremony in which everyone's voice is heard, not just that of the rabbi).

Indeed, the idea that made the most sense to me was respecting each other's beliefs—instead of creating a hierarchy of them or setting out to conquer or convert—because this was a step back toward the greater democracy and tolerance of pagan times in so-called pre-history. Then, the god of an ocean or a spring or mountain created a natural sense of awe in its presence, and each of us possessed a voice of god within us as part of our unity with nature.

After all, the withdrawal of god from women and nature had been a part of millennia that justified the conquering of women and nature. Given that history, everyone trying to honor and restore the feminine and therefore complete the universal—whether within an organized religion or outside it—is reversing the imposition of patriarchy and hierarchy. No wonder the antiwoman right wing of almost every organized religion, from the Christian ultra right in the United States to Islamic extremists in other countries, is in such violent backlash against the equality and power of women.

As Helen and I talk about our sense of a universal spirituality, she looks at me with bemused wonderment. "How did you ever get to be so full of love," she asks, "when you didn't grow up in a church or any religion?"

I look at her with the same wonderment. "How did you get to be so full of love," I ask, "when you grew up in one with a Son of God and not even a Daughter?" We both laugh.

Suddenly, it dawns on me that we are engaged in the same process: each of us is trying to salvage whatever was loving and welcoming, spiritual and universal, in our childhood experience. Each of us is seeking support for our belief in the connectedness of all living things.

We may have to rebel, enlarge and even transform structures as adults, but we choose not to discard everything. We cherish the words and phrases, the warmth and community, that have all the power of home.

Alice Walker expressed this cherishing in her poem, "Sunday School Circa 1950":

> "Who made you?" was always
>   The question
> The answer was always
>   "God."
>
> Well, there we stood
>   Three feet high
>   Heads bowed
>   Leaning into
>   Bosoms.
>
> Now
> I no longer recall
> The Catechism
> Or brood on the Genesis
> Of life
> No.
>
> I ponder the exchange
>   Itself
> And salvage mostly
> The Leaning.

Introduction

I had found my leaning in the back of Theosophical meetings. Helen had found hers in the warmth of a Texas Baptist church. Like the women of faith profiled in these pages, we wanted to add this to a new home that included our full humanity and that of the female half of the world. If we were to accept any exclusion—allow race, sexuality or anything that could divide up the human family—we would only create prisons for ourselves.

That's why we were sitting on the same couch, talking, listening, learning, leaning on each other, a microcosm of the warmth and community that is part of the worldwide women's movement. We were living proof of Helen's thesis that "relationship is sacred because the spirit of God is manifest in emphatic connection." If god is present in connection, then we must nurture it.

Now that a belief in an exclusive and superior afterlife for some people has coincided with Doomsday weapons, there could be no greater need to practice and cherish connection.

In this book, Helen has given us the stories of five women who inspire and connect with us in spirit. Her own story connects us with her life. We owe each other our honesty about spirituality. We owe our respect to feminists whose beliefs are different from ours. This book asks women of all backgrounds to sit together on the same couch, as Helen and I have done, and speak to each other with empathy and love.

LETTER TO THE READER

E*very childhood* is a dismantling of wholeness, and every adulthood is a process of putting the pieces together again. The search for connection to our wholeness is the overarching theme of this book and of my life.

Children's rhymes mirror the trauma of childhood, the shattering of Humpty Dumpty and the falling down of rock-a-bye baby. Yet as a child, I was sure that underneath it all, we were meant to be connected. I always intuited that the world was one large human family. My favorite pastime was reading the encyclopedia and thinking about how the cultural, biological, and historical details were all interrelated. And even today, I enjoy going to crowded places like Times Square, imagining how all of us—short, tall, male, female, dark-haired, tow-headed, from all over the world—are truly related to each other. An astute observer might suggest that my emphasis on connection probably comes from experience of its opposite. And that's true. I know what it's like to feel disconnected, on the outside, estranged, not only from other people, but also from myself. I spent many years trying to reassemble the fragments of my divided self and reconnect them.

Faith and Feminism emerged from an intuition that all life is interconnected and we are a minuscule yet crucial part of a massive design. We live in the midst of dissonance, rupture, and alienation. And yet there is gravitation toward unity that shows up in a variety of ways. Our religious faith and certain sociopolitical philosophies such as feminism are two of these pulls toward unity. To me there is no separation or conflict between faith and feminism. I am a feminist *and* a woman of faith. I don't feel any internal dissonance. But many feminists have an ardent mistrust of religion, and many women of faith have a strong aversion to feminism. Very often, my experiences in the women's movement have not supported this inner alliance between the spirit and the activist. Many consider feminism to be a secular movement with a bias against organized religion. While I understand why feminism has evolved this way, I consider it a deep loss. I also have met many individuals in the women's movement for whom religion is not a barrier. Like me, they do *not* feel the split between faith and feminism in their own lives. Working in the social and political arena is possible for them *because* of the sustenance and guidance they receive from their spiritual lives. When I talk to these women and work beside them, I feel awed by their tireless energy and their certainty that building a better world is possible. They speak openly about being empowered by their religious ideals.

My friend and colleague Dr. Olivia Cousins, a scholar, a Catholic woman, and a feminist, says: "As a Christian I am guided by the spiritual understanding that I am a steward of the world—responsible for the total well-being (mind, body, and spirit) of this planet." Largely because of my conversations with feminists of faith like Olivia, I began to feel that we needed a broader discussion of the vital connection between religious conviction and social action, the alliance between faith and feminism.

The more I thought about it, the more it became clear to me that religion and feminism are different expressions of the same impulse toward making life more just and whole. When we cut the connection between spiritual values and values of social justice, we weaken both our vision and our power. I believe there is an alliance between faith and feminism that, when allowed to find its natural connection, releases new energy for both.

My thoughts crystallized ten years ago when I was in a bookstore looking for a devotional book to take to a friend in the hospital. Nothing I picked up seemed right until I went to the biography section. There on the bottom shelf, dusty and in shadow, was a small book by Teresa of Ávila. I opened it and started reading. I had known Teresa was a woman of prayer, but I had never realized she was such an activist for women. I was astounded by her accomplishments. She seemed to me as great as any woman honored in the National Women's Hall of Fame. Why, I wondered, were there so few religious women installed in the Hall or celebrated in feminist circles?

I'll confess that my friend never got the book on Teresa. I kept it and soon after began to research Teresa's life. I knew I had to tell her story. I wanted to breathe life back into her memory. I felt convinced that her trials, her friendship with St. John of the Cross, and her courageous work for women in medieval Europe were stories relevant to women today. After months of reading, I began to imagine her life next to the life of early feminist abolitionist Sojourner Truth. As I put these two together in my mind, I became conscious of three more women of faith who were equally fascinating, and not widely discussed in feminist circles—Emily Dickinson, Lucretia Mott, and Dorothy Day. The "community" of these five women assumed a life for me and became the basis of this book. I knew they had important things to say to our world.

As a way of formalizing my interest in these women and others like them, I began course work at Union Theological Seminary, where I studied the lives of many women whose religious faith had ignited their social activism. I came across the Beguines,[1] a group of lay women whose work in the thirteenth century is considered by some scholars to be the first women's movement in Western history.[2] I went back even further to study the early church period. I studied a field called *patristics*, from the Latin word *pater*, or father, which introduces the fathers of the church. I also discovered a new field, *matristics*, which has unearthed stories of the many women who were early church leaders, most of whom have been left out of history.[3]

I began to take pilgrimages. I visited places where these spiritual women had lived, and I walked on soil where they had walked years before. I invited my husband, Harville, to accompany me to Ávila, where St. Teresa began her work of reforming the church in sixteenth-century Spain. My daughter Leah traveled with me to Bingen, Germany, to visit Hildegard of Bingen's monastery, where she and I wrote several ballads in Hildegard's honor.[4] We also went to France to retrace the steps of Joan of Arc throughout her heroic life. My son Hunter spent a summer in New York City working for the Catholic Worker, the hospitality house begun by Dorothy Day. On my way to visit my daughter Kimberly in Central America, I visited the Shrine of Our Lady of Guadalupe in Mexico City. I toured Marian shrines at Lourdes and Knock. I visited Black Madonna sites in Montserrat, Spain, and Einsiedeln, Switzerland.[5] My friend China Galland commented on how strange it was to see a Southern Baptist making regular visits to these Catholic shrines.[6] But I was moved by the power of this faith, which has inspired so much healing and social action.

The women I studied integrated faith and activism in a way I wanted to achieve in my own life. They were on fire with religious energy and used the flames to forge social change. They made important contributions to society, yet most are unsung heroes who are strangers to the women's movement. I want everyone to know their stories. These women could be considered our foremothers! Wanting to study women from other backgrounds, I began to delve deeply into writings of Latina, black, Jewish, Asian, and other feminist theologians.[7] Feminist theologians are modern-day prophets, calling us to a faith-fueled activism that has healing for our cultures.[8] They understand that religious as well as political and cultural institutions are calling for reformation, and that the spirit of God is central to all social transformation.

The concept of God resonates with diversity. My only regret about this book is that it is not as representative of that diversity as I would wish it to be. The women I write about are largely from the Judeo-Christian tradition. I have great respect for women who are Native American, or profess Islam, Hindu, or other faiths less well known or more personally defined. Had I written about them, my fundamental argument would be the same. But I believe that we speak most authentically from our personal experience. So I've chosen to write from within the Judeo-Christian practice, in order to illuminate the depth of my own tradition, which has at its core a sacred connection to all of life. My faith, and indeed the entire Judeo-Christian ethic, teaches love and empathy—two underdiscussed but essential aspects of effective social change. My tradition teaches: "I may speak with the tongues of men and of angels, but if I have not love, I am nothing."[9] What does this ethic mean for us as we struggle against injustice? I am writing, then, as an American woman, a Christian, and a feminist.

This book will introduce you to five women, who captured my attention years ago. These five—Emily Dickinson, Teresa of Ávila, Sojourner Truth, Lucretia Mott, and Dorothy Day—have become beacons for me. They may have been from different cultures and different centuries, but together they form a unified message. Each one lived beyond the gender expectations of her times and made significant contributions to the men and women who came after. The stories of these "spirited women" form the heart of this book. When you read about them, you will see that their religious and spiritual lives were indivisible from their public achievements. You can no more imagine them writing, giving speeches, or ministering to the poor without God's guidance than you can imagine their bodies functioning without their hearts.

Each of these women insisted on bringing their whole honest selves to their work. They were committed to prying open the rusty chambers of their hearts, and they inspire us to do the same. Emily Dickinson's story became a message about Pain, Teresa of Ávila's about Shadow, Sojourner Truth's about Voice, Lucretia Mott's about Action, and Dorothy Day's about our human Communion with one another. Each brief biography shows us how one woman was able to integrate pain, shadow, voice, action, or the expanded awareness of connection into her life and reach her potential as a human being. As I tell their stories, I will build an argument that it is possible for *us*, as individuals living now, to accept and integrate these five aspects of our being and experience. We too can move through the stages of pain, shadow, voice, action, and communion as we become more whole.

Because these women have been such a powerful catalyst for thinking more deeply about my own choices, I want to encourage you, the reader, to open yourself to the possibility of using these stories as a stimulus for your own life journey. My hope is that you will reflect on how pain has transformed you, whether you have claimed your shadow, if you have developed your own voice, how you take action, and the level of communion in your life.

As you read chapters 3 through 7 and learn more about these five women, you may wish to use a personal journal to reflect on how the issues raised relate to your own life. I've put together questions in the Continuing Reflection and Dialogue section at the end of the book that might help guide some of your thinking (see pages 143–162). In addition to your own reflection, some of you may benefit from reading this book with a friend or in a small group so that you can share your thoughts. Our relationships are the crucible of our greatest growth, and while you will be invited to move into "relationship" with these five women, you may also find it is an opportunity to deepen the relationship with a friend by doing this reflection together.

In Chapter 8, I share with you some part of my own journey from pain toward communion. My underlying goal is to encourage you to reflect on aspects of your own life and begin to form them into a story of who you are, where you've come from, and who you've met along the way. All of our stories are important, whether we've lived at the center of grand events or in the quiet of anonymity. Sharing our stories helps us see the movement of the spirit within our lives. If we don't tell our stories to each other, we lose the opportunity to find what binds us together, as human beings and spiritual beings.

The Afterword contains some thoughts about the future of feminism. I am impassioned about the women's movement and want others to understand and feel its potential. My vision includes both women and men in a movement that stands for the dignity and worth of all people, transcending the superficial differences of race, nationality, religion, gender, or social status. The truth is that we are all *already* sisters and brothers. We have only to recognize that truth and allow ourselves to be guided by its profound universal energy.

In ending, I return to the theme I started with—the theme of connection. I know with certainty that it is no accident that I am married to Harville Hendrix, who has written and spoken publicly for years about the subject of relationship.[10] Our mutual interest in the matter of connection began on our first date twenty-six years ago. An iconoclastic pastoral counselor when we met, Harville believed as strongly as I did in the power of relationship as a spiritual path. When we married, we agreed that our life work together would be to try to gain an understanding of the ways human history is propelled by human relationship, and to investigate the capacity of relationship to decode universal principles. Over the twenty years that Harville has encouraged the development and growth of Imago Relationship Theory, I was privileged to sit with him as companion and contributor.

Although Imago was developed as a way to restore broken connections within marriage, it can also help people understand and heal many different kinds of ruptured relation-ships within our culture. The spirit of Imago permeates every page of this book and is offered more overtly in the Reflec-tion and Dialogue section at the end of this book for readers who want to experience the process of dialogue. *We are meant to live in unity. We are meant to be interdependent. We are meant to be responsible for each other.* We need not the king's horses and men but do need *each other* to put ourselves back together again. This is the message of Imago, and this is the message of the lives of the five women in this book. If reading about them encourages you to think about the connections in *your* life, then I will have accomplished my goal.

Chapter 1

To Build a Dialogue

Attempting to bridge secular and faith-based feminism is very important. Women of faith feel that the rights movement is anti-religion, and the rights activists haven't made enough effort to listen to and include the women of faith. The social justice movement needs both voices. We need to be able to move to the next step, of dialogue between the rights world and the religious world.

—Dorothy Q. Thomas

In past decades, many of us have been aware of a gulf between faith-based and secular feminism. On one side were activists who found religion indispensable to their activism. On the other were activists who found religion outdated, superficial, or perhaps just irrelevant to their activism. While on a personal level, there was some interaction between these two groups, an occasional casual friendship, on the philosophical level, there was a barrier. If a feminist happened to refer to her spiritual life in "mixed company," she was likely to be met with an embarrassed silence. But if she talked exclusively from a secular point of view, she was using the lingua franca of the movement, and nobody would raise an eyebrow.

Dorothy Q. Thomas, founding director of the Human Rights Watch Women's Rights Division and a 1998 Mac-Arthur Fellow, has spoken eloquently about this division and the need for healing through dialogue. I agree with her. More women in the movement are looking for ways to reconnect and reintegrate secular and faith-based worldviews into a single, stronger feminism. In order to bridge the gulf, we need to consciously create opportunities to talk and to listen. Dialogue gives us a way to find common ground.

In 1995, I found an opportunity to engage in dialogue with women about faith and feminism. In the spring of that year, I was preparing to attend the United Nations Fourth World Conference on Women in Beijing, China.[1] It seemed to me that the conference was a once-in-a-lifetime opportunity to hear from women from all over the world about important issues in their personal and social lives.[2]

I decided to interview conference participants about their thoughts on religion and the women's movement, and developed a survey consisting of three open-ended questions. The questions were designed to encourage my interviewees to share their personal experiences regarding religion and feminism. Originally, I had hoped to interview women from all over the world, but as I thought about it, I focused only on women from the United States. I had a hunch, which was later confirmed, that women from other countries might not split their faith from their feminism the way we do in the United States. My questions to American women were simple. Was the social activism of secular women and faith-based women unified and coordinated? Did they experience a split between the two? And if so, *why* was there a split? What should be done about it? I didn't know it then, but these questions became the impetus for this book.

The results were striking. *All* of the fifty women I interviewed said they felt a polarization.[3] Not one of them thought that secular and faith-based feminists were working in coalition or in harmony with one another. As they talked about the reasons for the split, many said that while spiritual matters were important to them personally, organized religion had been no friend to women. The institutionalized church has been one of the fiercest opponents of women's social and political equality. One of the women I interviewed put it most graphically: "Of course feminists shy away from religion. There is blood on the cathedral steps."[4] She was talking about the blood of women sacrificed because of the church's doctrinal traditions.

She was right. The historical record of the church includes too many examples of women's oppression and too few documenting support for women's rights.[5] I understand why feminists might want to stand apart from these male-centered ideologies and theologies. Why be a willing participant in an organization that has acted in opposition to its own core teachings on the equality and worth of all human beings?

3

If you are like me, this is a question you have asked yourself. All thoughtful people of faith must come to terms with the church's damaging contradiction between principle and practice on the subject of women's rights. I have wrestled with it for many years. Because I was raised in a Christian family, my spirituality has been nurtured within the Christian tradition. But I had to learn how to maintain integrity while practicing allegiance to a faith that I knew was deeply flawed when it came to being expressed in daily practice.

I admit to being led first by my heart in these matters. I love my faith. The beauty of the ritual and liturgy reminds me of the oneness of the entire human family. My faith makes clear to me that equality and justice are not just social constructs, but an ontology, part of the divine order of life. That we are all a part of a large web of connection that is sacred, if we have eyes to see.

For me, the brainwork comes later, after the love. Nevertheless, the brainwork has to be done. In order to be a Christian and a feminist, I must understand and reconcile apparent opposites. This reconciliation takes place within me every single day as the seeming contradictions of my faith and my feminism actually amplify and enlarge, even complete one another's core values.

What I know to be true is this: the crimes of any religious institution do not negate the value of universal love and the religious ideals at its core. Sadly, human institutions will always be flawed reflections of the values they hope to embody. Every women's organization falls short of its values and ideals as well, and the work of feminism is to name these ideals and to strive for them. If there is blood on the cathedral steps, we must also recognize the bloodshed inherent in combating political oppression. If we are so angry at the deeply flawed parts of religious institutions that we cut ourselves off from our spiritual birthright, we make no gains. Instead our anger is exacerbated by profound loss. I say preserve the anger, yes, but also preserve our right to our spiritual traditions. The patriarchy may have stolen our freedoms, but we don't have to be complicit in the abandonment of our souls.

Two Revolutions: Feminism and Religion

When I talk about Christianity and feminism, I do so with the awareness that each is a whole complex world of ideas and feelings. Although I am clear about the ways they are different, I see them springing from the same originating impulse. Both are revolutions of consciousness, a manifestation of the desire and need for inclusion and connection.

Early Christianity shook up the established order of life under Roman rule by proclaiming that freedom and grace belonged to *everyone.* Nearly two millennia later, early feminism (the 1830s) emerged with a similar message and made it more specific and inclusive. Then the second wave of feminism (the 1960s) articulated the message once and for all through the proclamation of the National Organization for Women,[6] which defined feminism as "the radical notion that women are people."[7]

These two revolutions of faith and feminism, though very different, were built upon the same fundamental assumption:

every person is intrinsically as valuable and worthy of love as any other.
The implications of this revolutionary doctrine are stagger-
ing. Both Christianity and feminism did more than suggest a
few fresh ideas to the prevailing worldview. They shook
things up until a new world order emerged. The new Christian and the early feminist could see the kingdom of justice
and equality for all was just within reach.

In their dynamic, pure form, both of these revolutions
sought to enlarge our capacity for compassion and empathy.
Both preached the transformation of the human mind and
heart, and both have contributed to the evolution of new social orders. On a personal level, each of us separately can reflect on whether our experiences with Christianity and
feminism have felt congruent. Have our feminist experiences
been Christian? Have our Christian experiences felt feminist?

Feminism

I wanted to take some time to study the origins of American
feminism, and in so doing, accidentally stumbled upon the
abolitionist feminists of the nineteenth century, whose relatively unknown story needs to be told. These were women
of color as well as white women, who knew that their country was founded on the ideal of "liberty and justice for all,"
and decided to take this declaration at face value. They took
offense at the idea of a liberty that was for white men only.
The same rights belonged to men and women of color, to
poor people, to immigrants, to children; all humans were de-
serving.

The story begins with a fierce band of Quaker women who

began to ponder the unequal treatment of women and people of color in the culture. In the silence of their meetings, a voice spoke to them and guided them to the work they needed to do in the world. They developed absolute certainty that God's law demanded freedom for all people. Slavery must end. They were confident that *they* were being called by God to bring this vision of justice into the world. No more taxation without representation. No more pay discrepancy. No more silence in the church. They tucked their Bibles under their arms and marched to the first abolitionist–women's rights meetings, propelled by the vision of this spiritual mandate.

Increasingly, scholars acknowledge that American feminism was rooted in the abolitionist movement, and that religion played a central role in condemning the institution of slavery and substantiating the need for immediate abolition. Women created many local female abolitionist societies. Representatives of these societies came together in New York in 1837, forming the Anti-Slavery Convention of American Women, the first national political women's meeting in America's history. Both black and white women met and began to break the taboo of speaking in public and petitioning in the political arena. Calling their work "the cause of God," this courageous band of 180 women saw themselves on a mission to unite Heaven and Earth, in the form of a society that would live and practice the democratic and religious ideals it espoused.[8]

This convention has received relatively little study by historians. But the documentation of this meeting shows these earliest feminists to be revolutionaries and visionaries who had their eyes on a universal law that superseded man-made ecclesiastical and governmental laws of the day. I studied these earliest feminists for two years, focusing on how they were galvanized by their religious passion to act in radical revolution. They were catalyzed into action not by a social ethic, but by a belief in an ontology of connection—that we are all meant to live in equality and harmony. It was this metaphysical vision that set fire in their hearts and started a social revolution. Having the conviction that something needed to change meant doing whatever was required. "This is a cause worth dying for," declared Angelina Grimke about her commitment to speak out against slavery.[9]

The backlash against women meeting together publicly was severe. When these same women met again the next year, this time in Philadelphia, a mob of 10,000 men encircled the building, shouting and angrily throwing stones through the windows. It got to the point where no one inside the meeting hall could hear what was being said. When it was impossible to continue the meeting, the women filed arm in arm out into the street. While they were able to exit safely, the mob continued to riot around the meeting hall, breaking the doors and windows. They finally set fire to the building.

This public backlash to the women's convention was devastating in some ways but also galvanizing in others. Reading the women's diaries and other primary accounts of this event, I could feel the deepening resolve of these early feminists. It came naturally, from the deep springs of their faith in God. The women documented the proceedings of each convention, and these writings help us see how their faith and their courage to fight for social reform were intertwined. They began their meetings with prayer. Then they voted on public resolutions such as this one: "The time has come for woman to move in that sphere which Providence has assigned her, and no longer remain satisfied with the circumscribed limits with which corrupt custom and a perverse application of Scripture have encircled her."[10] This statement is the first public call for women's rights in America.

I can't read these words without feeling stirred. And I find the phrase, "a perverse application of Scripture," to be a startling acknowledgment that the ecclesiastical structures of the day used religion as a weapon against women, especially against those who were fighting for the professed ideals at the heart of Christianity. This is not an unknown tactic in our own time. I am often embarrassed or outraged by fundamentalist doctrine that, in my view, has been used to set back the progress we've made in human rights. We must continue to be wary of the "perverse application of Scripture" for the purpose of justifying policies and institutions that keep people divided and excluded.

As I studied this early feminist organizing, I saw it was significant in other ways. The abolitionist feminists insisted on "Sympathy for the Slave" as the organizing motto. They worked in pairs, circulating petitions, and in groups on collaborative writing projects. And in so doing, they acknowledged their awareness that their abolitionist activism brought the values of empathy and relationship they had cultivated in their homes into the public realm. They had no intention of leaving behind the strengths and beliefs they knew would serve them well as they enlarged the sphere of action. Empathy and relationship—two values desperately needed in public life today.

Ten years later, in 1848, what is generally acknowledged to have been the first women's rights meeting in America was held. Five women met in Seneca Falls, New York, for what became a notorious tea party where women plotted revolution. The women were Elizabeth Cady Stanton, Martha Wright, Jane Hunt, Mary Ann McClintock, and Lucretia Mott. They shared their outrage over not being allowed to participate in public meetings or have a voice in society. The decision was made at this small but historic meeting to place a notice in the newspaper calling for a Women's Rights Convention to be held at a nearby church. The purpose would be "to discuss the social, civil, and religious condition and rights of Woman."[11] The notice ran on July 14, 1848, and only five days later, three hundred people, including some forty men, attended the first Women's Rights Convention. About a hundred attendees signed their names to the famous Seneca Falls Declaration of Sentiments and Resolutions, written by Elizabeth Cady Stanton. Some of the same women attending this convention had helped plan the antislavery conventions, and their knowledge of protocol helped to make this gathering a great success. This Seneca Falls Convention is considered to have officially set in motion the most important social movement of America's history.

In her memoirs, Elizabeth Cady Stanton states that there was "a religious earnestness that dignified all the proceedings."[12] While this meeting laid the groundwork for what became the suffrage movement, in truth, the movement's social implications were broader than that. By starting with the issue of the vote for women, they were ushering in a social transformation that cut across the political, social, and economic structure of the country. Think of it! Five religious women sitting at tea, believing simply that God had called them to do the right thing, were catalytic in a groundswell movement to usher in social equity that is still reverberating in our lives.

It is remarkable that one of the most significant social revolutions of all time was fueled in large part by the personal convictions of a small band of nineteenth-century religious revolutionaries. I don't think we can begin to understand their actions if we don't make an effort to understand their faith. Nor can we understand their faith without looking more closely at their lives.

When we read their letters and study their public writings, we learn an interesting fact. Nineteenth-century feminists made a distinction between institutional authority and their own intensely personal religious experiences. The fact that the church wasn't supporting their efforts didn't mean that God wasn't supporting them, nor did it invalidate their religious faith. Those early feminists were filled with the confidence that their mission was an outgrowth of divine order and justice. They sorted out the issues wisely. Personal religious experience is not necessarily the same as organized religious doctrine. My concern is that as contemporary women we have lost the capacity to make this distinction. As far as I'm concerned, if a religious institution does not support an issue that is based upon Christ's teaching, it's imperative to challenge the institution, not necessarily the teaching.

Unfortunately, some feminists are immune to this difference. They have thrown the proverbial baby out with the bathwater. They have ignored the transformative power of religion because they deplore the stupidity and blindness of some of its practitioners. And many contemporary feminist historians have written the history of the women's movement solely from the point of view of the secular academy. They have not entered into the reality of these earlier feminists, nor truly listened to their words. This, combined with the fact that churches and temples have been among the strongest opponents of the women's movement, has created a vast chasm between faith and feminism.

Religion

As a political movement, feminism seeks to transform society by challenging and changing social institutions. Religion, on the other hand, seeks first to transform individuals through a personal relationship with God, which then results in a desire to work for the transformation of society. Religion and feminism share many common ideals.

Someone with a religious sensibility develops an acute awareness of certain questions. Do I live out my beliefs? Am I the same person in public that I am in private? Am I experiencing life as it is, delicately interconnected? Am I working from anger? Am I working from love? I know many women in secular feminism who function from this same place of integrity, but the religious feminists I know have an advantage.

Their faith requires and supports the continuous exploration of these questions, and their communities of faith are there to help them find their way when the journey becomes difficult. In order to talk about religious qualities as more than abstract ideas, let's explore how they become manifest in individual people. By listening to the voices and understanding the lives of women of faith, we will be able to see whether religion has enlarged or restricted their potential. From my study of the early feminists, it is clear to me that religion was far more to them than a source of comfort. It offered a process for integrating disparate experiences and provided a source of empowerment and transcendence that made these women giants. On a personal level, these early feminists overcame being called misfits and heretics by recognizing that, in the larger view, they were extremely important to God. In them, self-examination and self-acceptance occurred in the same moment. They presumed themselves to be incomplete, but they knew they were accepted in their incompleteness and loved anyway. And this is the optimum mind-set for anybody who wants to undertake the hard work of social change.

As the women in this book show us, faith and feminism can work together to achieve the same ends. Both Christianity and feminism offer a prophetic vision for the future by inviting the transformation of the individual and of society. The two may be experienced differently, but they point us in the same direction.

This understanding was brought home to me at an annual fund-raising breakfast for the New York Women's Foundation, one of over a hundred women's funds that make up the Women's Funding Network. After the program, Florence Pert, an associate minister of Marble Collegiate Church, approached me. "You know what's really going on here, don't you?" she asked. "This isn't just about coming together to pool resources for women's causes, the way it's talked about. This is about church."

As I reflected on her comment, I began to understand what she meant. We each contribute to the split between faith and feminism when we think of them as dualities. Social action is as much an expression of the spiritual impulse as are prayer and ministry. Women's funds include those who are marginalized and left out of the rooms of power. They give voice to those who are voiceless. They reach out to women who are in prison because they carried drugs for their boyfriends. They provide material help to inner-city mothers struggling to work and care for their children. Florence Pert carries the belief, as do many women of faith, that whenever we act for the common good, we are engaging in spiritual action. Feminist activism fostering justice, equality, and love embodies the prophetic, powerful verse in Scripture: "Let justice roll down like waters . . ."

Healing the Split

In the twentieth century, feminism developed in opposition to religious authority and became a secular political movement. It has sponsored an honorable political agenda and achieved significant improvements in the economic and social lives of millions of people. But in this great work, the renewing, transformational language of the spirit has been obscured.

The women's movement has not found a way to reconnect comfortably with the religious impulse that was central to its origin. Ironically, we have emulated the male model of progress through separation rather than connection. Feminist social scientists, especially those at the Stone Center at Wellesley, have written about the female pattern of development, which, given that the mother and daughter have the same gender, emphasizes the importance of remaining *in relationship*. This is distinct from the male pattern, which encourages separation. [13]

The feminist movement has not been able to stay in relationship with religion. We couldn't have separated faith from feminism more completely if we had been agents of the patriarchal system separating the concept of love from the concept of power. Will such separation continue to serve the larger purposes of the feminist cause? This is an important question for each of us to consider personally.

The severe secularism of the twentieth century appears to be softening, but a dangerous extremism also appears to be growing. More people now tend to talk about matters of the spirit, but as feminists and people of faith, we must acknowledge efforts to use religion as a political vehicle to compromise our human rights. Our task is to call upon the passionate faith of the abolitionist feminists that generates within us a moral courage, that moves us toward social justice, and that opens us to our indissoluble relationship to God and to each other.

There is growing interest in examining the point at which the political and the spiritual intersect. Service to others *is* a spiritual value, and the overt recognition of this can be part of the development of our own wholeness. My hope is to add my voice to the chorus of other women who are calling for a bridge between the secular and the spiritual. Our effectiveness in building this bridge will depend on how well we connect to each other in every interaction. That means taking the time to listen to those who come from points of view that are different from our own. If we listen well, learn from one another, and find the ability to empathize with one another's experiences, I believe the split will have served us well. When a broken bone mends, it becomes stronger along the break. When we strengthen our connections to one another, we become whole. And when we are whole, we are empowered and can empower others.

Chapter 2

The Journey Toward Wholeness

The personal is political

—ROBIN MORGAN, *THE ANATOMY OF FREEDOM*

F*or the women* who jump-started the second wave of feminism in the 1960s, this simple sentence was a rallying cry. It was a declaration that feminism would work toward healing the division in our souls both in the public and private realms. It was a declaration of the importance of wholeness.

The early, or first wave, feminists I mentioned in the last chapter were troubled by the ethical contradictions they saw around them every day. The country espoused democratic and Christian principles of liberty and justice for all, and yet over half of the men in Congress owned slaves. Women were not allowed to speak in public, much less hold office. The abolitionist feminists rose up demanding a greater congruence between public declaration and private living. And in the second wave, Robin Morgan's words were a particularly succinct summary of this call to congruence. In one simple sentence, feminists of the time forged a link between private and public that has been a guiding principle of the movement ever since.

Think about what this coalescing of public and private has meant in your own life. Child care is not a personal problem for working mothers to solve as best they can. Child care is a political and economic issue with implications concerning who can earn money and become independent. Similarly, we all agree that it isn't enough to vote against domestic violence. We have to abolish—to declare as unthinkable—domestic violence in our personal lives. It is important to achieve congruence between our public statements and our daily living. The women's movement, built on the idea that "the personal is political," should never want a woman like myself to separate her personal from her political. So I work alongside others to bring women of faith into the feminist fold. Clearly, we must strengthen an internal dialogue that will allow us to accommodate our differences and strengthen our public voice at the same time. But besides talking and listening to each other, I suggest that we can enrich our understanding of each other with biographical story.

I learn so much from stories of women from other times and places. I am particularly interested in their struggles, their motivations, and their ingenuity. In seeing the courage in their hearts, my own heart grows stronger. I have spent some years reading biographies of women who integrated religion and social activism. For these women, creating a division between the secular and the spiritual would not have made any sense. Far from being a detriment to their personal and political development, religious energy was the fuel that ignited their purpose and their activism. The question that fascinated me was: how did religious faith catalyze their power?

I wanted to understand how these dynamic women were able to find their purpose in life and pursue it fearlessly. In their ability to live in service to a larger vision, they seemed to embody a new definition of holiness.

Holy Women

In my own mind, I began to think of these women as "holy women." I am aware that this phrase seems to set them apart as different from or better than the rest of us—and this is not my intention. Certainly, they were not ordinary, but neither were they from a different species. They were flesh and blood like we are. That's why their stories have power—because we can identify with them. Our common humanity opens the channel between us.

Among other things, we see how they struggled with the same issues we have. I suspect that it has always been difficult for people—both women and men—to find their own river in life and to draw deeply from their own waters. Some of us never find the course of our own lives, and others of us may find it, only to be repeatedly caught in currents of personal desires and obligations that pull us in divergent directions.

My readings by and about holy women brought me into contact with women who have managed to steer their own course better than most. What I learned was that they did not need to separate their faith from their feminism. There is a sweep of grace that moves these holy women from believing, to voicing, to doing, to being. Every one of them felt as if she had a direct connection with God. They didn't just *believe* in the possibility of personal revelation, they *experienced* it, powerfully and unforgettably. The revelation occurred at least once during each of their lives and in some cases over and over again. When I read about their experiences, I got a sense of what it would be like to experience God directly and know that God had chosen me for a special purpose: "Fear not: for I have redeemed thee. I have called thee by name. Thou art mine." Those words of the Hebrew Scriptures rang true in their lives.[1] They have made me consider the possibility that I—and you too—have been chosen, without our knowledge, for a special purpose.

I noticed also that these women were remarkably determined. When they were discouraged, they plowed ahead anyway. They were pigheaded, convinced that they were *in the right*. They felt released from many of the petty conventions that governed the behavior and thinking of the people around them. Direct, personal communication with the divine, whether mystical or not, liberated and empowered them. It may have put them in service to God's commandments, but through this commitment, they discovered a profound freedom.

Authentic religious expression for them was an experience of the soul and made no distinctions of gender. As Lucretia Mott said, "In Christ, there is neither male nor female."[2] Gradually, I have realized the core of what set them apart for me. It is that they lived, more than most of us, from a place of wholeness. They were authentically themselves without amputations or edits.

"Holiness" and "wholeness" are near homonyms. But looking beyond their similar sound, I find that allowing myself to muse about these two words brought to mind enriching associations. Most important, "holiness" is a religious word, and it is religion that promoted the wholeness of these women as individuals. Through their own personal communication with the divine, they experienced what it was to be loved. Love is above all else an acceptance of the whole, including flaws, the "holes" in us, so to speak. Holy women have a faith that reveals the strength of vulnerability. Their openness to a relationship to God and to others gives them their depth.

These words then, "wholeness" and "holiness," are relevant to feminists as vibrant words that connect us to our strength and power. As we work toward our own wholeness as individuals, we are working toward the wholeness of feminism as a social movement. The stories of the five women that are the heart of this book offer clues for each of us about how we can find our own wholeness.

Choosing the Five

I have to admit that I am drawn to the five women you'll soon meet mostly because of their remarkable stories—epic stories, each one. But, in addition, they represent a spectrum of nationality, ethnicity, and time: Emily Dickinson, a nineteenth-century New England poet, who resisted organized religion and society only to become a mystic; Teresa of Ávila, a feisty sixteenth-century Spanish reform-activist nun; Sojourner Truth, an escaped nineteenth-century slave who ultimately earned both spiritual and political freedom; Lucretia Mott, a demure-looking nineteenth-century Quaker, who took pride in being called heretical; and Dorothy Day, a twentieth-century Catholic revolutionary, who is about to be designated a saint, a fact she would hardly find credible. Though each woman represents a different perspective and background, the common taproot of faith grounds them all.

I have fallen in love with these five women. Because my thinking has been shaped by theirs and my feelings have expanded in their company, I feel intimate with them. Reading their stories has led me to learn more about my own story, and this has poignantly authenticated the saying that "one woman's story is all women's stories."[3] We are each part of a stream of people whose private thoughts are really variations on general themes. We experience with writer Mary O'Reilley that "the universe knows our song."[4]

These women are well known. Scholars and historians have documented their lives and achievements. I reread their stories, curious about the source and the fuel for those achievements. I have found them to be friends on my own travels and hope they will become your friends as well.

The Five Stages on the Journey Toward Wholeness

Think of the hero's journey as perceived by Joseph Campbell. The mythical hero, usually an unlikely male, undertakes a physical journey to an unknown land. On the way, he is faced with a series of challenges that he can meet only through his superior physical strength and cunning. If he succeeds in getting through all the barriers, he wins the prize, which he can then take home for the benefit of his people.

Although this model has some application to the experience of women, it is not adequate to describe what a woman must do in order to live beyond the stultifying expectations of the culture in which she's raised. If she has small children, she can't take a trip or move to a new place, and very rarely is she called upon to beat down her opponent with force. Instead, her journey is an inner one where the demons are her demons of the self. Her task as the heroine is to return from her inner journey and share her knowledge, wisdom, and energy with the people around her.[5]

Each of the five women profiled in this book represents one aspect of the internal journey of the heroine. Each of their stories teaches us what we have to do to meet a particular developmental challenge before we can move on to the next one. Their life stories reveal how they learned to face their fears and overcome external obstacles, and how each lesson made them stronger.

Let's envision the model of these stages of personal evolution as a circle, albeit a flexible rather than a rigidly constructed circle. Personal change does not happen according to a neat chart. The stages, then, are not really separate, but are dynamic and in motion. In life, these stages run into each other. As we go through these stages, we are sometimes self-confident and at other times self-questioning. But once we come to a critical understanding of that stage, we can integrate the lesson to be learned. In the journey to become whole, a woman will be confronted with various forms of these stages. In doing the hard work that is required, she learns important lessons about herself and increases her capacity to see the meaning of her actions. She is then able to bring more experience, wisdom, and skill to the next challenge she must face.

Here is a brief summary of the five stages that we will follow in the lives of the women in this book. Although each woman progressed through all five stages, she exemplified one stage in a particularly vivid way. The stages are:

1. **Pain.** Emily Dickinson's life teaches us that embracing the pain in our lives can be the doorway to deeper meaning and purpose.

2. **Shadow.** Teresa of Ávila's life teaches us that integrating shadow aspects of our personality allows us to learn from all parts of ourselves, making us stronger and more whole.

3. **Voice.** Sojourner Truth's life teaches us that when we are able to speak our truth we gain a new "name," a new voice—that is, a new empowered self-concept and identity.

4. **Action.** Lucretia Mott's life teaches us that once we have found our true voice, it's time then to act and to bring our values into the world in a concrete form.

5. **Communion.** Dorothy Day's life teaches us that as we move into an expanded awareness of connection, our ultimate work is toward communion, mending connection in the world.

Although these women lived in different periods and under very different circumstances, a common narrative thread unites them. Taken together, they illustrate the five stages on the path to wholeness. Each one of these women's journeys began with pain. Experiencing pain, accepting it, and learning from it, is their initiation into a way of living that would lead them out of the particular and into the universal. These women, like many of us, experienced personal suffering, but like fewer among us, they also attained the power to alleviate the suffering of others. I think a key to attaining this transformation can be found in the depths of these five developmental stages.

Each story is an account of the transformation of the personal self to the expanded self, from individual concerns to social concerns, from private life to public life. For these women, private experience became the gateway to the path of compassionate understanding. They could not make a deep and powerful connection to the larger world until they were able to connect to themselves.[6] And, in an example of the kind of feedback loops that characterize all living systems, they were not able to connect to themselves until they were in authentic relationship with others. To me, the vibrating energy that connects two or more entities into one relationship is the spirit of God in the world. It is in this sense that living becomes a form of worship. Early feminist Emma Goldman reminds us of the importance of dancing *together:* "If I can't dance, I don't want to be a part of your revolution." Whenever we move together within the intricate dance of relationship, we experience the divine.

On the outside, holy women appear to be very different from each other, but on the inside they are all fed from a common spring of spiritual insight. The underlying order in their wild and disparate lives is their religious faith. Belief in God is the organizing principle around which their personalities and biographies coalesced.

Like oceans, we ebb and flow and are in constant motion. We have a deep desire to keep things as they are, and a contradictory desire to expand beyond our current limits. Times of relative equilibrium allow us to build the strength we need for times of movement. It can be difficult for us to know which stage we are in and whether we are moving forward at all. But underneath our seemingly individual current, we are ultimately being pulled forward toward a connection with the greater whole. These stages make it clear why connection is the theme of this book. Each stage helps us become more connected—inward to our inner selves, outward to other people and the social issues that move us, and upward (so to speak) to God. As you read the stories in the next five chapters, I hope you will pause often to think about how what is happening in the holy women's lives is relevant to yours. Think about how their early uncertainties, as well as their small and significant steps forward, relate to your own. As you traverse these women's life paths, reflect upon your own goals and achievements personally, professionally, and spiritually. Imagine yourself in conversation with them and invite them to respond to whatever questions you might have.

Chapter 3

EMILY DICKINSON
1830–1886

Claiming Your Pain

There is a pain — so utter —
It swallows substance up —
Then covers the Abyss with Trance —
So Memory can step
Around — across — upon it —
As one within a Swoon —
Goes safely — where an open eye—
Would drop Him — Bone by Bone.

—EMILY DICKINSON, POEM #599,

"THERE IS A PAIN SO UTTER"

E*mily Dickinson experienced* a great pain in her life, which became a frequent subject in her poetry. We do not know the source of the pain, yet it is clear that she allowed this hurt to become an opening into the depths of her heart.

And from out of the depth, she sent back messages of great courage and honesty. Even as she pulled back from society, she felt a need to communicate with the world. Given the expression of talent preserved in the wooden trunk at the foot of her bed—1,775 poems and fragments were found at her death—it was clear that Emily was connected to an inner wellspring that manifested itself in a prodigious poetic vision. She is now considered the most widely read woman poet in the twentieth century. Her courage to make this journey and her extraordinary ability to capture the experience of pain with words are models for us today of how pain can become a transforming agent in our lives.

"Bulletins from Immortality"

Emily was born in 1830 to a New England Calvinist family. All but one year of her life was spent in Amherst, Massachusetts, an affluent community of God-fearing Christians. As an adult, she lived with her parents and took care of them in their old age. When she did venture out of the house, she usually wore white.[1] Her neighbors called her the *"phantom of Amherst."* This public perception of Emily's life seems so contrary to the literary giant she became.

Emily's father was a prominent politician who expected his children to unquestioningly take up his beliefs and values. Contrary to Emily's introversion, her mother led an active social life. Given how immersed she was in thought and prose, it seems inevitable that Emily felt disconnected from her parents. Her letters reflect this. In one of them, she wrote of her father, "He buys me many Books—but begs me not to read them—because he fears they joggle my Mind." And about her mother, she wrote, "[She] does not care for thought."[2]

Emily's formal education started at Amherst Academy. Then she attended Mount Holyoke Female Seminary, where, despite her successful academic life, she stayed only seven months. We do not know why she returned home so quickly. Nor why she never ventured far from home again.

Given Emily's unwillingness to function more actively in a social context, she doesn't seem to fit the stereotype of a feminist in action. You might wonder why she is included among the five empowered women in this book. It is important to remember that not all feminists are activists, and I am including Emily as an opportunity to expand what it means to be a feminist. In her daily life, she was shy to the point of being a recluse, while in her writing, she revealed herself with a level of honesty that took enormous bravery. Her life is an example of the richness that can be found when one follows one's deep inner voice rather than conforming to societal pressures.

This is a quality that Emily shares with other feminists who stayed on their own path despite the pressures of the status quo. Her life and her words make a unique contribution to the chorus of women's voices. They remind us that there is room for all of us in our uniqueness. There is no one kind of feminist. There are times in life when we may withdraw or set firm boundaries to protect our inner life and experience. The purpose of this is often to gain the strength and knowledge we need to communicate on a deeper and more honest level.

For these and other reasons, Emily is an embodiment of

"the personal is political."[3] At the age of seventeen, Emily firmly upheld her own feelings about organized religion. At one point during religious instruction, Emily's teacher divided the class into three groups: The Christians, the "Hopers," and the "No-hopers"—those for whom there is absolutely no hope. This teacher then asked all those who wanted to be Christian to stand. Emily was the only one who remained seated. Emily's refusal to stand with the Christians resulted in her being the only one in the group of the "No-hopers." Later she wrote, "They thought it queer that I didn't rise; I thought a lie would be queerer."[4]

By not rising, Emily resisted yielding to group consciousness, remaining boldly planted in her own sense of authenticity. Often when we hear of someone resolutely fixed in their own will, we envision a dominating person with an imposing presence. Yet that picture couldn't be farther from the description of Emily by Thomas Higginson, the well-known poet and editor, who wrote of his first meeting with her: "A step like the pattering child's in the entry and in glided a little plain woman with two small bands of reddish hair & a face a little like Belle Dove's, not plainer—with no good feature—in very plain and exquisitely clean white piqué. . . ."[5] Emily described herself as "small, like the Wren, and my Hair is bold, like the Chestnut Bur—and my eyes, like the Sherry in the Glass, that the Guest leaves."[6] Eyes are often described as the window to the soul, yet Emily described hers as something left over, abandoned by someone not willing to take that very last sip.

When she had accumulated a sizable number of poems, Emily looked for advice as to the possibility of publishing them anonymously. This is how, in 1862, she found the editor Thomas Higginson. Higginson recommended that she standardize "her rough rhythms and imperfect rhymes" as well as her spelling and grammar. He felt that the public would not appreciate her gift if its form were not "corrected."

Emily refused to compromise her writing style and made the difficult decision not to publish. As is well known, part of the uniqueness of Emily's poetry is expressed in her odd spelling, word usage, and particularly her punctuation. What enabled this diminutive "Belle Dove" to follow her own counsel? In her lifetime, God and pain were her companions. Feeling their constant presence, she was able to forge a profound inner life that fueled a remarkable literary output.

Perhaps one of the most baffling questions about Emily is: what led her to her self-imposed isolation? Scholars have studied this but to this day still have no answer. While we have only fragments of the facts surrounding what this painful experience might have been, her poetry clearly expresses the intense grief she felt. Some scholars speculate it was a rejection in a love affair, and others suggest she may have been in love with a man or a woman her father forbade her to see. What we know is that some great psychic assault catapulted her into this lifelong hibernation. And that the depth of her grief gave her an authenticity that vibrates through her poetry, transcending the specifics of cause.

Emily is like a brave explorer reporting back to us from a new land. Yet once we hear her words, the familiarity she describes awakens us. In poem after poem, she traversed the psychic landscape within, charting the terrain with uncanny attention to nuance. Struggling to decode the mystery of her inner pain, she poured her findings like liquid fire on the page:

> After great pain,
> a formal feeling comes.
> The nerves sit ceremonious like tombs. . . .
> This is the hour of Lead
> Remembered, if outlived
> As freezing persons recollect the snow.
> First the stupor, the chill, then the letting go.[7]

The pain led to a sense of utter hopelessness, as Emily expresses in the following lines:

> Doom is the House without the Door—
> 'Tis entered from the Sun—
> And then the Ladder's thrown away,
> Because Escape—is done—[8]

Emily did not allow this hopelessness to deaden her feelings. Instead, she used it to deepen her experience of grief. Her descent through pain offers us a glimpse into the mystery of a world bereft of light, as alien and fascinating as the ocean depths yet so common that we wonder if she can read our minds. Through her words, murky images come into focus, as if part of some great awakening. In this way, her poems become a celebration of feeling. She did not shun life as much as she shunned the nonlife and the hypocrisy she witnessed around her. Emily understood that pain and joy are eternally mixed—and that each can be accessed through the other.

Emily is a model of a woman who made herself whole by retreating to her deepest, darkest personhood. Through accessing her pain, she created holy ground, a sacred stillness. Within that stillness she discovered an authentic divine connection. In time, she began borrowing biblical references to seed her own visions. She became high priestess of her own religion, wedded to God, formulating her own unique relationship. This impulse anticipates the democratization of religion, which fuels in our souls the unleashing of all human potential.[9] Emily drew upon the power of communion with the divine essence, taking it into her own being, writing, "Given in Marriage unto Thee. . . . Oh thou Celestial Host—."[10] Emily was frail and insular and yet connected to a source of great power. She illuminates for us the potential to be fearless explorers of ourselves: to watch, listen, and accept what we find without the biases the world can often impose.

Throughout her lifetime, Emily experienced transcendence in the mundane and glory in paradox. "Consider the Lilies," she wrote to a friend two years before she died, "was the only commandment I ever obeyed."[11] She was known to end a prayer with the words "In the name of the Bee / And of the Butterfly / And the Breeze—Amen!"[12] Emily charted her own spiritual life, based on the truths she carefully cultivated from the authenticity of her poetry. She created her own rites of passion, death, and resurrection. Hers was a maverick but profoundly felt religiosity. She was a precursor of the feminist theologians today who call for a re-creation of a relevant theology that mirrors the existence and experience of women.

Emily's poetry charts an evolution from avoiding pain to

claiming and being defined by it. Pain shapes us, breaking us open so that we can reconfigure ourselves in a way that more deeply mirrors our authentic self. "There is always one thing to be grateful for," she writes, "that one is one's self and not somebody else."[13] In this way, she celebrated her selfhood in the midst of her suffering, a profound teaching for us all.

Emily teaches us that pain opens us not only to deeper levels of our self, but also to the humanness of others. She wrote, "When Jesus tells us about his Father, we distrust him. When he shows us his Home, we turn away, but when he confides to us that he is 'acquainted with Grief,' we listen, for that also is an Acquaintance of our own."[14] She wrote about feelings we avoid, and her unique spirit of feminism encourages us to give voice to our own lives, to find the power in emotion, and to trust it as a way of connection. When we work through our own grief, we can cut to the heart of the common universal experience, which opens us to feel for others.

From Emily, we also learn that pain grounds us and is necessary for the formation of integrity. Her poems evoke being reduced to one's foundation, cut to the quick by grief until what is exposed is bone-honest essence. For Emily, pain was an essential part of the creation of her fundamental self. Pain branded her and strengthened her spirit. She poured her vulnerability into her poems, understanding that her own experience was all she could offer.

This paring down to her barest essence connected her to the universal source of life. "The only News I know / Is Bulletins all day / From Immortality."[15] Her definition of faith included her doubts. She wrote about her conviction:

"... we both believe, and disbelieve a hundred times an Hour, which keeps believing nimble."[16] And with this nimble but electrifying belief, she ultimately was able to claim:

Take all away from me, but leave me Ecstasy,
And I am richer then, than all my Fellow Men—
Ill it becometh me to dwell so wealthily
When at my very Door are those possessing more,
In abject poverty—[17]

Emily Dickinson was a survivor. She was willing to sit still and offer a presence for the pain and suffering within. She also embodied the wisdom of the sixty-first hexagram of the I Ching, which is the hexagram of Inner Truth: "Though one abides in one's room, words are well spoken, they are felt at a radius of a thousand miles."[18] We feel the truth of her words and respond on a deep, instinctual level.

Only ten of her many poems were published during her lifetime. After she died, her sister and Higginson collaborated to "correct" her verse; they published Emily's first book of poems in 1890. In 1891, and then in 1896, two more "corrected" editions were published. The world had to wait until the 1950s to enjoy Emily's unedited poems and letters.

Emily Dickinson died of Bright's disease—kidney failure—on May 15, 1886. Her last letter, written a few hours before her death to her young relatives, speaks from the spiritual hinterland where she lived and died: "Little Cousins. Called Back. Emily."[19] Emily's work has endured because in it, she gave voice to our experience.

Pain as an Agent of Transformation

Our society runs from pain. And as a feminist, I want to be especially careful when writing about the subject of pain. The history of women has been the history of a destructive kind of suffering, and I do not suggest moving further into that experience. My point is that walking away from pain altogether is equally as destructive. The debilitating suffering comes when we do not allow ourselves to feel and work through our pain. Facing pain honestly and surviving gives us strength. By opening to pain, we allow it to become a transforming agent—the kind that fueled Emily's prolific works.

Kathleen Norris, in her work *The Cloister Walk*, explores pain's role in individual transformation. She tells us that "both lamentation . . . and exultation . . . can be forms of praise."[20] She then references Emily's insight that "Pain—is missed—in Praise," which speaks to woman's impulse to make a quick jump from the experience of pain to spiritualize it or gloss it over. When women disavow pain or close their eyes to the violence directed toward them, they keep themselves from using pain as a catalyst for action.

Pain can be a doorway to access a larger consciousness. Like the psalmist, we say, "Take me to the place that is higher than I." We move away from a fused experience of suffering to a place of enlarged understanding, where we, like Emily, integrate our pain into the fullness of our life.

Emily withdrew to sit with her pain and discovered a universe within. She experienced a new liberation. She celebrates this internal life of freedom in these playful lines:

I'm Nobody! Who are you?
Are you—Nobody—too?
Then there's a pair of us!
Don't tell! they'd banish us—you know!

How dreary—to be—Somebody!
How public—like a Frog—
To tell your name—the livelong June—
To an admiring Bog!²¹

Though we do not have to withdraw from the world as she did, Emily reminds us that at times we need to be remote in order to explore the richness within. I watched my daughter Leah struggling to fit in with her peers during junior high and high school. She made a decision to stay home alone in her room rather than spend social time with teenagers, with whom she had little in common. While sitting with her pain, she began to paint. These paintings are now hanging throughout our home and are reminders of her willingness to sit quietly with her experience.

Pain offers an arresting context that humbles and deepens our perspective. In a society that holds up doing and achieving as primary, we all need to take a cue from Emily to withdraw in moments when we feel anguished. Her existence, characterized by quiet patience and self-possession, expresses the Scripture in Luke 21:19: "In your patience, you possess your soul." We are all the richer when we stop, like Emily, to find a quiet place to explore the layered life that lies beneath the surface.

Η ΑΓΙΑ ΘΕΡΕCΙΑ ΤΗ ΑΒΙΛΑ

ST. TERESA OF AVILA

Chapter 4

TERESA OF ÁVILA
1515–1582

Integrating Your Shadow

Amid Squalls, my love
In shrinking, my growth
And in loss, my gain.

—TERESA OF ÁVILA, "LET MY JOY BE IN LAMENTING"

The journey toward wholeness requires decisions that are conscious and intentional. However, we also develop through hidden or unconscious forces that influence our journey without our full awareness. The hidden, lost, or rejected parts of ourselves can be called our "shadow."[1] For me, Teresa of Ávila is an example of a woman who was able to integrate all parts of herself, even her "shadow parts," into a formidable personality. Teresa came from a simple Spanish family, spent most of her life sequestered in a convent, and for many years suffered from debilitating illness. While she did not have the benefits of formal schooling, she produced a body of writing that led her to become "the most widely read Spanish author next to Cervantes."[2] She became a model of a lived spirituality, whose activism was noted by her contemporaries, one of whom said, "Teresa de Jesus has done more for the Order than all the friars of Spain."[3] By facing and befriending her shadow self, Teresa opened her own depth to discover the power of a faith-fueled life.

A Young Woman of Charm

St. Teresa is one of the most important women in the history of the Christian Church. Her canonization in 1622, forty years after her death, was fraught with controversy because as a powerful leader of reform, she had challenged many traditional doctrines of her day. For example, she dismissed what some held up as the Pauline injunction that women be silent in the church. She also developed a new, spontaneous form of prayer, challenging the traditional recitations. In her lifetime, she founded seventeen convents, encouraged the foundation of eighteen monasteries, and was "the only woman of the Church ever to reform a religious order of men."[4] In all, her books and written reflections total more than 1,000 pages, and her letters (450 remaining extant) add up to another 1,000 pages. In 1970, the Roman Catholic Church proclaimed her a Doctor of the Church, which means, among other things, that her writings are taught as part of church curriculum. She was the first woman in history to be given this distinction.

Early biographers, intent on her canonization, white-washed the biography of this complex woman. Skimming over controversial aspects in her life, they presented her as deeply religious throughout her life. It is only in recent years that historians have brought to light the richness of her multivalent personality, including the probability that she was of Jewish lineage and the fact that one of her brothers was born mentally disabled, both marks of shame in Spanish society. What is clear is that Teresa's greatness is a direct re-flection of her capacity to embrace and integrate her com-plexity. Today we would describe her as a woman who has "done her shadow work."

Born in 1515, Teresa lived during the height of Spain's golden age, the sixteenth century. During this time Spain was the most powerful country in Europe. Gold and silver from Mexico and Peru made Spain richer in currency than all the rest of Europe combined. The churches in Spain were adorned with great art; they developed elaborate rituals and gained worldly prestige.

Teresa was raised in the small Spanish town of Ávila. She was a highly spirited child. In her autobiography, we learn that her mother died when she was fourteen. She was devas-tated by the loss but boldly turned to adopt the Virgin Mary as her spiritual mother. Yet even with this internal spiritual mentor, Teresa gravitated to rebellious adolescent activities. She seemed aware of her charming personality and enjoyed her passion for boys and dances. Flamboyant and flirtatious, she reveled in the bright colors of her baroque Spanish homeland, loved reading romance novels, and had a burning desire for adventure and martyrdom. In writing about her early years, she noted her love of clothes and bragged that her favorite color was burnt orange. She once said, "I have no defense against affection; I could be bribed with a sardine."[5] In addition to her outgoing personality, she was a chess-player, skilled horsewoman, and excellent dancer. Yet Teresa later wrote about feeling considerable guilt over the way she had spent her youth, having lost what she considered were "the good habits" of childhood. Some contemporary biographers suggest that she "acted out," like a rebellious teenager. Her father sent her to live in a convent because he knew of no other way to give her structure.

"Cut Out Nothing About My Sins"

At the time, Teresa fought this decision. The alternative to life in a nunnery was marriage. But the thought of becoming a submissive wife to a dominating husband did not appeal to her rebellious spirit. Moving into the convent, she struggled with this dilemma until she found that life there was not so oppressive. Her religious readings lit a fire to a growing love for God. Eventually, she acknowledged that she had shared her father's concern: "I knew I was in the hand of danger. . . . They put me in a convent in the neighborhood where they took care of girls like me, only not so evil in their ways."[6] Inner conflicts from her adolescence manifested outwardly as various forms of illness and she spent months at a time in bed.

After two years in the convent, she returned home to help care for her younger brothers and sisters. She stayed home for the next three years. But the life of the convent, which she had at first despised, now called to her. She decided to join the Carmelite Convent of the Incarnation. In 1535, at the age of twenty, she entered the Carmelite order, where she was to remain for the rest of her life.

In sixteenth-century Spain, women had little opportunity for meaningful lives outside marriage, except as members of religious orders. While convents were often filled with dissatisfied young women, it must also be said that convent life empowered women in many ways. A convent was an acceptable place for women to be free of many of the social constraints of the time.[7] However, Spanish Catholicism at this time had become synonymous with social prestige. Therefore, the convent experience was a mixture of both pious and social elements, a mirror of Teresa's own inner conflict with her shadow.

The convent where Teresa lived allowed visitors, and she had a steady stream. For many years, her beauty and her bold conversation made her a magnet for male attention, both from laymen and men of the church—something she enjoyed. Eventually, however, the convent's emphasis on money and status began to bother her. She became increasingly disturbed by the salon atmosphere of the Carmelite convent, even while she was drawn to it. Her order followed all the liturgical formalities, but Teresa knew that the frivolous social interaction she and others engaged in was at odds with the spiritual life of poverty and contemplation on which the order had been formed.

Teresa felt pulled in opposite directions. As one of her biographers noted, she was "a vain and vivacious girl with a divine agenda."[8] She did not want to abandon either her pull toward sacred issues or the passion she had for the world. She wanted it all; she wanted her wholeness, and she kept the two passions in tension with one another. In her autobiography, she wrote about the anguished struggle being waged in her soul:

> I can testify that this is one of the most grievous kinds of life which I think can be imagined, for I had neither any joy in God nor any pleasure in the world. . . . I do not know how I managed to endure it for a month, much less for so many years.[9]

For the next eighteen years of her life, Teresa found herself trapped in an inner war that she described as a "battle and conflict between friendship with God and friendship with the world."[10] She wrote of being drawn to one of the male attendees of the convent's salon. We don't know his name, but it is clear that her friendship with him generated more inner struggle. Her advisors counseled her to focus her mind on God, but she knew she had to be honest about who she was and work with the fullness of her being.

During this time, it became difficult for Teresa to practice prayer: "I tried as hard as I could to keep Jesus Christ present within me. . . . My imagination is so dull that I had no talent for imagining or coming up with great theological thoughts."[11] She admits there were some years that she did not even attempt to pray, finding it almost impossible: "I was more occupied in wishing the hour of prayer were over . . . than I was to remain there. I don't know what heavy penance I would not have gladly undertaken rather than practice prayer."[12] She became seriously ill during this time and wrote of her agony and her confusion. Teresa wrestled with her shadow, and ultimately brought all her feelings before God. A priest had advised Teresa that in writing about her life, she minimize her personal problems and struggles. She ignored him, trusting that God wanted all that she was and had a use for every thought and passion in her being:

> I don't believe that I exaggerate much when I say a
> thousand times, though it may start a quarrel with the
> one who ordered me to play down the account of my
> sins—and mightily prettified, it is all coming out! I beg
> him for the love of God to cut out nothing about my
> sins, for it is just there that the glory of God is shown—
> by what He will put up with in the human soul.[13]

Over the years, Teresa persevered in her inner struggle until she finally was able to integrate her love of God with her natural desire to please. She eventually evolved a new way to pray: "frequent solitary converse, with Him who we know loves us. If love is to be true and friendship lasting, certain conditions are necessary: on the Lord's side, we know these cannot fail."[14] Once she had this realization, she was filled with a passion to live out her prayer life in her daily experience. Her deeply personal, intimate relationship with God opened in her a deep well of confidence and joy. Her life became dramatically effective. Having worked through pain and darkness she began to live from joy rather than fear. When new nuns were being interviewed, she asked that they not be brought in if their reasons for joining were fear-based. When she saw a timid nun, she was known to roll her eyes and say, "God deliver me from solemn saints."[15]

In 1554, at the age of thirty-nine, Teresa underwent a conversion experience triggered by a vision of Christ. From then on, she was able to choose one direction: a life of prayer in action. As she prayed, she used her body as her instrument. Moving beyond the cerebral reciting of prayers, her whole being would become suffused with overpowering seizures of holy joy:

> It was the first time the Lord had given me the grace of raptures. I heard these words: "Now I want you to talk no longer with men, but with angels." It threw me into amazement, for that whole movement of the spirit was so great, and those words spoken so very much within the spirit—and so it frightened me. Yet, in another way, it brought me comfort that stayed with me after the fear.[16]

Teresa had made progress integrating her shadow self into a whole, impassioned person. She soon became a leader within her community. Teresa decided that the most powerful form of prayer was prayer in action. Aware of the ways Spanish convents were lax in the area of spiritual discipline, she started a reform movement. Her purpose was to found new convents that supported a dedicated life of prayer. In 1562, she founded the first of seventeen convents of Discalced Carmelites ("shoeless Carmelites"; the nuns wore rope sandals).

Though Teresa knew herself to be an instrument of God, the church hierarchy in and near Ávila considered her delusional and dangerous. They doubted that her public visions, raptures, and even levitations were evidence of God. Some said it was demonic possession. The Catholic authorities became even more uneasy when she set out to reform the Carmelite order using her unorthodox form of personal prayer. Six times she was denounced by the Spanish Inquisition. She survived the attacks on the validity of her work, because her efforts were imbued with love as well as revolution.

Teresa never doubted the authenticity of her connection to God. She was certain that her trances were the result of the divine union that fueled her work. Her self-assurance drew others to her and helped her create a large following as she traveled around Spain. Teresa's spiritual sisters encouraged her to write and share her wisdom with novices. She began writing her autobiography, a story that has galvanized both women and men for almost five hundred years. In it she writes of the "Four Waters of Prayer," an allegory for the progressive stages of the spiritual life. The "Four Waters" describes the orchard, *el huerto*, as a metaphor for the soul, which becomes barren if left unattended but if cultivated is able to produce luscious fruits and fragrant flowers.

In the beginning of the "Four Waters," the gardener (Jesus) pulls one bucketful of water at a time from a deep well in order to water the orchard. Each bucket represents prayer for the soul. She writes that such efforts "will mean advancing at the pace of a hen," yet over time this "First Water" results in the barren soil of the soul becoming more moist and potentially productive. In the "Second Water," a shift begins to occur. Prayer life becomes more natural, as though a windlass or pulley aids the gardener so that water is drawn with much greater ease. By the "Third Water," the gardener has dug irrigation ditches that enable the garden to flourish. In the "Fourth Water," God sends a downpour of rain. A person who reaches this Fourth Water receives an outpouring of grace from the heavens. Teresa understood the arduous task of cultivating the barren field in the soul. It takes effort and discipline, but the result is a sense of abundance, grace, and deep love.

Teresa is remembered not only for her writings but also for founding a new order of nuns within the Carmelite tradition. In the process of instituting her reforms, she persuaded a Carmelite friar of the ancient order—who in time would be known as St. John of the Cross—to join the reform. He became the first Discalced Carmelite father. Two years before her death, the Discalced Carmelites received papal recognition as an independent monastic body. Teresa died in Alba de Tormes on October 4, 1582.

Her influence continues today within the Carmelite Order of Nuns itself, which currently has 65 monasteries in the United States and some 600 worldwide.[17] The more recent Teresian Order founded by St. Henry de Osso in 1876 currently has 209 communities worldwide.[18] In addition, she has inspired countless people, including Edith Stein, a celebrated philosopher and author who was recently canonized by the Catholic Church, and who said the most influential person in her life was Teresa of Ávila. Teresa's vibrant image so inspired Dorothy Day that she named her only daughter Tamara Teresa.[19]

Integrating Your Shadow

Teresa's story dismantles the common belief that all those chosen for sainthood are flawless in personality and character. Indeed, she would want us to consider her contradictions and struggles as integral to her sainthood. When I read her spiritual writings, I can see that she was worried at various times in her life by her own conflicting nature. She often wrote, "I am crossing myself as I write this." Teresa's ability to acknowledge all parts of herself has been an inspiration to me. She traversed the spectrum of human emotion, and found herself to be flawed, but trusted God to accept all of her. Her vulnerability and openness led to her empowerment.

Teresa was able to work within the imposed structures of the church and articulate a faith that was both uniquely hers and recognizably Catholic. In doing so, she transcended the limitations of her circumstances and became a universal figure.

Like Teresa, each of us is a mix of unseen strengths and conflicting desires. While it is easy to understand our suffering in terms of external difficulties, most of us aren't aware of the significant role we play in our own difficult dramas. Like Job, we rail against the heavens for sending us trials at times, while in actuality, our own shadow is our most formidable opponent. One of the keys to living deeply is to learn how to befriend our shadows instead of demonizing them.[20]

Our shadow side often connotes our negative qualities. These can be identified easily. Whenever we feel irritated by someone, chances are they are doing something that causes similar but hidden parts of ourselves to react. These aspects of ourselves are important to acknowledge.

Before we had the language of psychology, people talked about their "sinfulness" as a barrier or distraction to living in harmony with the divine order. The Christian tradition even has its own way of identifying some shadow character traits. The Seven Deadly Sins are a description of the negative aspects of shadow—pride, greed, lust, anger, gluttony, envy, and sloth—prior to their being integrated. As long as they remain unidentified, they can take a variety of forms, including an unhealthy prioritizing of luxury, the fear of social disapproval, or a chain of broken relationships.

One way to respond to these "sins" is found in *The Divine Comedy*, in which Dante is ultimately led to the vision of God by his guide, Beatrice. In first traversing through the Inferno, Dante reveals that the inhabitants of the Inferno are not there because they are sinners. Sinners also make up the populations of Purgatory and Paradise. Rather, those souls are in the

Inferno because they are sinners who refused to admit to their own sins. They denied their faults and projected them onto others, blaming everyone around them. The lesson we learn is that only when our sins become acknowledged and deeply felt can they be integrated. Deep reflection and prayer are an important part of the integration of the shadow. Once we admit to our shadow with honesty and an open heart, the shadow has the potential to become transformed.

Once the shadow is integrated, the Seven Deadly Sins can become aspects of a healthy self. Greed and lust become passion, imbuing our journey with heart and fire. Anger transforms into righteousness that acts compassionately for our own and others' behalf. The healthy side to gluttony is self-care, something many women have to learn. Envy, once integrated, becomes an appreciation of others. And in a society where doing is valued over being, sloth turns into the ability to be still. Pride enables us to feel good about our accomplishments and grow in confidence and strength. But the path to authenticity is to admit these qualities are within us. It is shadow work that enables holy women to make their hidden struggles into levers with which to free themselves.

Shadow characteristics can become detriments or assets. It depends on whether they remain hidden and unexamined or are accepted with vulnerability. Teresa's story illuminates the path of courageous self-acceptance that leads to the open heart.

Chapter 5

SOJOURNER TRUTH

1797–1883

Finding Your Voice

Her speech had operated on the roused passions of the mob like oil on agitated waters; they were, as a whole, entirely subdued, and only clamored when she ceased to speak or sing.

—THE NARRATIVE OF SOJOURNER TRUTH

The *search for voice* is the search for self. The Hebrew God, Yahweh, made the same unassailable statement of beingness: "I am that I am."[1] Voice is an expression of each person's unique "I amness." Sojourner Truth was a nineteenth-century slave who became an activist, working tirelessly on behalf of freedom, dignity, and equality for all. Though she was born into slavery, her courage to claim her God-given rightful place began when she declared: *"I am"*—self-owned, self-defined, and self-asserted. For a woman, much less a woman in slavery, this was a terrifying thing to do. Claiming our voice, and our selfhood, is a sacred act. And it was this sacred act that launched Sojourner on a journey that began when she gave herself a new name, and took her to the doors of the White House, where she brought her activist work into the political arena.

"So Shall Truth Be My Abiding Name"

How Isabella Hardenbergh became Sojourner Truth is a story that illustrates the transformation of silence into full-throated voice. She spent her childhood bearing mute witness to the pain around her. As a young adult, she hid behind a twig wall where she whispered her prayers to God. She didn't learn English until she was twelve years old—her first language was Dutch—and she never learned to read or write. Yet, by the time Sojourner died, she was a nationally celebrated activist who spoke vehemently and unapologetically against many forms of oppression.

Isabella began life as a slave, one of humanity's most silenced creatures.[2] Her owner stopped by the day she was born, "just long enough to notice that his new possession was a healthy, long-limbed girl with shining blue-black skin."[3] From that day forward, she was known as "Colonel Hardenbergh's Belle."

How did this illiterate black female slave find her voice? Sojourner's life exemplifies the process that occurs within ourselves as we grow to understand that we hold the authority to shape our own lives. This inner authority came when she embraced all of herself, which enabled her to speak from an authentic voice. Sojourner literally spoke herself into being.

Born in New York State around 1797, Belle was the daughter of a deeply religious woman, Mau-Mau Bett,[4] who sang songs she learned at her own mother's knee. She would talk to her children about a "Mighty Being . . . who hears and sees you." "Where does he live?" Belle asked one day. "High in the sky," her mother replied. "When you are beaten or cruelly treated or fall into any trouble, just ask him for help. He will always hear and help you."[5]

Years later, Belle told the story of how she was put on the auction block when she was nine years old. Torn from her mother, Belle turned to the source of comfort her mother had given her years before. Since slaves had no privacy, an adolescent Belle built a wall made out of twigs. She didn't think her prayers would be heard unless they were spoken aloud. So she hid behind the wall to voice her thoughts. In this quiet place where she could speak her mind, Belle felt safe and protected. God was real for her, and she found solace and strength in His presence.[6]

Belle's faith gave her strength to endure the iniquities of bondage through almost twenty-nine years under four different masters. During her enslavement, she was partnered with a fellow slave and bore five children. With each child, the pain of enslavement intensified. It broke her open, rending a hole where a flash of insight shone. Belle realized that God was everywhere in everything. "There was no place where God was not," she proclaimed. She felt God transformed from an all-powerful masterlike being into a mystical presence that infused all life. "Who are you?" she cried. "At length an answer came to her, saying distinctly, 'It is Jesus.' 'Yes,' she responded, 'it is Jesus.' "[7]

This realization strengthened Belle's inner voice. What began as a whispered prayer to God became a crystallized understanding that she and her children deserved to be free. At the break of a new day, in 1826, she ran away from her owners and was reborn into freedom. She took her baby daughter, born that same year, with her but was forced to leave her other children with their master. The family with whom she sought refuge gave her lodging and helped her purchase her freedom. She was able to remain in contact with her other children, and when they were freed, she was finally able to provide them with a home of their own in Michigan.

During her first years of freedom, Belle cleaned houses and was also called to do Jesus' work among the poor and disenfranchised in New York. One day, while on her hands and knees scrubbing a kitchen floor, a message came to her: "I am no longer Isabella."[8] Looking down at her callused hands, she realized that while her body belonged to Belle, her spirit had changed. It was time she stopped being a servant—paid or not—to white folk. From now on, she would only do the work of the Lord.

On June 1, 1843, a forty-six-year-old Belle left New York. By her own determination, she was a pilgrim of the Lord, a free woman. And her old name would not do:

My name was Isabella; but when I left the house of bondage, I left everything behind. I wasn't going to keep anything of Egypt on me, and so I went to the Lord and asked him to give me a new name. Oh God, give me a name with a handle to it, oh that I had a name with a handle. And it came to me at that moment, like a voice as true

Sojourner Truth: Finding Your Voice

as God is true, "Sojourner Truth," and my heart did leap for joy. Sojourner Truth, why, I said, thank you God, that is a good name. Thou art my last Master and thy name is Truth. So shall Truth be my abiding name until I die.[9]

Naming herself was an act of taking authority. By claiming her freedom and renaming herself, Sojourner came into full voice.

Armed with her new name, Sojourner embarked on her God-appointed journey, which resulted in her becoming a powerful figure in the nationwide struggle for the abolition of slavery, the recognition of women's rights, the rights of freedmen, temperance and prison reform. It could be said that her role as speaker and reformer officially started the day she came across a huge outdoor religious meeting. Intrigued, she moved to the edge of the crowd and realized that anyone who had something to say could speak. Compelled to voice her experience, she approached the podium.[10] The crowd stilled at the sight of the imposing six-foot-tall black woman. In her deep voice, she told of her first meeting with Jesus and spoke of the poor she had served in New York. Breaking convention, Sojourner finished with a song:

We are going home; we soon shall be
Where the sky is clear, and the soil is free;
Where the victor's song floats over the plains;
And the seraphs' anthem blends with the strains.

After the meeting, she was surrounded by those enthusiastic about her message, eager to mirror back the truth she

59

had voiced. This was the first of countless meetings Sojourner attended throughout her life. She never failed to include a song or two. She was described by those she encountered as a tall, dark woman with searching eyes, a powerful voice, and an original turn of speech walking through town after town. In time, word of her arrival preceded her, and she drew a crowd wherever she journeyed.

The more she spoke, the more her faith matured from an awareness of her own pain into a relational awareness that the system of slavery had to be abolished. She traveled around the East and Midwest, voicing her belief that slavery was an abomination and not condoned by God. She continued to put her voice and her message into song:

> I am pleading for my people,
> A poor downtrodden race,
> Who dwell in freedom's boasted land,
> With no abiding place.
> Whilst I bear upon my body
> The scars of many a gash,
> I am pleading for my people
> Who groan beneath the lash.

Sojourner's voice was the instrument that enabled her to claim her full self. Once she had done this, she was able to use her instrument and life story to help gain freedom for others. An editorial covering one of her speeches captures not only the depth of her gifts, but her impact: "One of the most unique and interesting speeches of the Convention was made by Sojourner Truth, an emancipated slave. It is impossible to transfer it to paper, or convey any adequate idea of the effect it produced upon the audience. Those only can appreciate it who saw her powerful form, her whole-souled, earnest gestures, and listened to her strong and truthful tones."[11] Think back to the context when this editorial was written. Most women had little social or legal existence in society. It was extremely rare for a woman to speak in public, especially a black woman. But Sojourner refused to be silenced, and echoes of her thundering voice still reverberates today.

In the summer of 1850, Sojourner was asked to be the Massachusetts delegate at the first national Women's Rights Convention. Women's rights was a new and startling concept to everyone. At the convention, her first reaction was impatience. The other women in attendance, all upper-middle-class, had privileged lives far removed from Sojourner's firsthand experience of slavery. They were demanding the right of a woman to keep her jewels and silver if she chose to divorce her husband. After listening for a while, Sojourner questioned: "Sisters, I'm not clear what you be after. If women want any rights more than they've got, why don't they just take them and not be talking about it?"[12]

As the convention progressed, however, Sojourner began to feel a kinship with these women. She felt Lucretia Mott's anger at getting half the pay of male teachers and empathized with the stance of one of the convention's organizers: Lucy Stone declared that she wouldn't take her husband's last name in marriage because he wasn't her master. These women were demanding a political voice. Sojourner took fire as an activist for both abolition and women's rights.

In 1851, at a women's rights convention in Akron, Ohio, Sojourner gave perhaps her most famous speech. Standing at the podium in all her commanding dignity, she is reported to have said:

> That man over there says that women need to be helped into carriages, and lifted over ditches, and to be in the best place everywhere. Nobody ever helps me into carriages, or over mud-puddles, or gives me any best place! And aint I a woman? Look at me! Look at my arm! (and she bared her right arm to the shoulder, showing her tremendous muscular power). I have ploughed, and planted, and gathered into barns, and no man could head me! And aint I a woman? I could work as much and eat as much as a man—when I could get it—and bear the lash as well! And aint I a woman? I have borne five children and seen them all sold off to slavery, and when I cried out with my mother's grief, none but Jesus heard me! And aint I a woman?[13]

Unsurprisingly, many attempted to silence such a forceful critic of slavery and sexism. In 1858, in Silver Lake, Indiana, a hostile audience attempted to shame her into silence. Some men claimed that she was too vigorously outspoken to be a woman and demanded that she give proof of her sex. She did as she was asked, baring her breast in public, a gesture that turned the shame back on her tormentors. Once she found her voice, nothing and no one was ever able to silence it. She was even humorous about it. When a white man told her that her speeches would not accomplish anything, being no more important than a flea bite, she answered, "Maybe not, but the Lord willing, I'll keep you scratching."[14]

Fueled by an expanded passion to create social equality for all, Sojourner continued her travels, embarking on a formal lecture tour. Her voice boomed throughout the gatherings as she insisted that the work had to be seen in its whole context: "There is a great stir about colored men getting their rights, but not a word about the colored women; and if colored men get their rights, and not colored women theirs, you see the colored men will be masters over the women, and it will be just so bad as it was before. So I am for keeping the thing going while things are stirring; because if we wait till it is still, it will take a great while to get it going again."[15]

Sojourner's voice had the power to incite or calm a crowd. Disgusted by a frenzy that erupted at one meeting, Sojourner was the only speaker who wasn't afraid to approach the podium. "Hear! Hear!" she cried, "Are you not commanded to 'watch and pray'?"[16] At another meeting, she couldn't remain silent when a minister maligned the cause of women's rights. "That little man in black there [pointing to the minister], he say women can't have as much rights as men, 'cause Christ wasn't a woman! Where did your Christ come from?" The crowd went wild. "From God and a woman." She then shot a withering look toward the minister and boomed, "Man had nothing to do with him." Sojourner concluded: "If the first woman God ever made was strong enough to turn the world upside down all alone, these women together ought to be able to turn it back and get it right-side up again. And now that they are asking to do it, the men better let 'em." I imagine her voice was like the trumpet that the second writer of Isaiah described in the beginning of Chapter 58: "Shout out, do not hold back! Lift up your voice like a trumpet! Announce to my people their rebellion. . . ."[17]

The need to express her God-given truth propelled Sojourner on her tireless crusade well into her sixties. In 1864, Sojourner knocked on the doors of the White House, where she pushed for an audience with President Abraham Lincoln. She knew that with the nation's leader's seal of approval, her work would gain wider acceptance. When a meeting was finally arranged, Sojourner admitted to President Lincoln, "I never heard of you before you were talked of for President." Lincoln replied, "Well, I've heard of you, years and years before I ever thought of being President. Your name was well known in the Middle West."[18]

Sojourner remained in Washington for many years, where she counseled the freed slaves who poured into overcrowded slums. In 1865, she was appointed director of the Freedmen's Hospital of Washington with the words "give her all facilities and authority." She pushed herself beyond all limits of age and body, working for the emancipation of blacks and women.

Sojourner Truth died at her home in Battle Creek, Michigan, on November 26, 1883. She had cultivated her inner voice behind a wall of twigs when her faith led her into a quiet stillness. Sharing her story and speaking her truth to others, she developed her outer voice, encouraged by those who listened to her. The claiming of her whole voice transformed her from a slave called Isabella into a spiritual pilgrim who helped bring America into alignment by proclaiming God's vision of the world. With uncommon strength and passion, she broke through the chains of bondage that had held her tongue captive, and in so doing, inspired millions to forge a new path of equality for all.

Finding Your Voice

Harville and I took our son Hunter to Washington. Standing in front of the Lincoln Memorial, I told them the story of Lincoln's respect for Sojourner. I'll never forget how we imagined the two of them in conversation and marveled at how Sojourner had found such voice. Voice is an important aspect of wholeness. Feeling our pain moves us into shadow, where we reclaim denied parts of our selves. This leads to developing a voice that grows increasingly more authentic and fullthroated with each newly claimed aspect of our identity. We are no longer speaking from a foundation of self that is riddled with fault lines. The more unified we are, the more authority our voice contains. We voice ourself into being.

As we know, there have been many historical periods when women were barred from public speaking, but claiming that they spoke for God gave women both confidence and authority. Sojourner Truth was explicit about her divine mandate: "Children," she would thunder at the beginning of her talks, "I talk to God and God talks to me." Imagine how much more closely her audience listened to this large, impressive, fearless preacher because she said straight out, "I have come to tell you about my direct communication with the Lord."

While women have come far in their ability to speak on their own behalf, there are many women who compromise what they want to say and what they actually say. Almost all women experience a dissonance between inner and outer. As a matter of emotional and sometimes physical survival, women have found it necessary to split their speech into two parts. One kind of speech is suppressed, occurring only in safe settings with intimates or within the ultimate safety of a woman's own mind.

The second kind of speech is the publicly acceptable type that conforms to social expectations. The injunction to suppress certain feelings or thoughts can be so powerful that a woman may not be aware of it and may honestly believe that publicly acceptable speech is all she has in her. Carol Gilligan's work describes the destructive effects of this splitting of voice, especially in young girls who, as they embark on adolescence, have trouble speaking with clarity and strength.

An emphasis on listening cultivates a stronger expression of voice. Listening is a crucial component in Imago Theory, where couples are taught to mirror, or repeat back, each other's thoughts, feelings, and needs as a way of building not only their partner's sense of self, but their own. Our core self becomes stronger when it is mirrored back. Voice that is not mirrored dies. When the process of mirroring is followed by validating and empathizing, a deep listening is done with feeling. All of us need validation—that who we are, what we think, and how we feel does make sense. And the deepest form of listening is empathy, by which we are able to resonate on a soul level with the feelings and needs of one another.

A wise proverb states that "Speech is silver, Silence is

gold," reminding us of the forgotten value of silence. Feminist theorist Patrocinio Schweickart chose those words as the title of her article on talking and listening that parallels the inward and outward rhythm of Imago dialogue.[19] She points our attention to the value of quiet as a tool that helps us notice the complex interplay of inner and outer that characterizes any creative process. For something new to happen, we need silence and receptivity as well as action and productivity. While some theorists see speaking as active and listening as passive, Schweickart and Imago Theory both point to the reality that both speaking and listening are active. Listening is a way of meaning-making. Theologian Nelle Morten refers to this dynamic as "hearing each other into speech."[20]

Ultimately, the development of authentic voice is a process that involves a flow between speaking and listening. In listening, one becomes attuned to the surroundings so that speech becomes relevant and meaningful. This undulating rhythm of speaking and listening is the bedrock for dialogue in Imago Theory and for all of us who care about relationship.

The holy women in this book undertook the journey to find their voice with God as their partner. They discovered that they had to listen in silence before they could speak from the divine source within them. It was in listening that their voice developed power. Throughout their lives, they sought periods of solitude and communication with God out of which emerged their voices of authority. In this way, their voices carried a power that has given their words relevance through the ages.

Chapter 6

LUCRETIA MOTT

1793–1880

Taking Action

I long for the day my sisters will rise, and occupy the sphere to which they are called by their high nature and destiny.

—LUCRETIA MOTT, Sermon: "The Truth of God . . .
The Righteousness of God"

God has a special purpose in mind for each of us—and the only way we can fulfill it is by *doing*. Lucretia Mott had little patience for theorizing and philosophizing; she transformed her beliefs and feelings into concrete daily actions. Born into the Quaker tradition and grounded in the values of honesty and integrity, this ordinary woman, small in build and plain in speech, but mighty in courage, became a radical activist for justice and peace. Perhaps her most no-

69

table distinction came in 1923, forty-three years after her death, when the first Equal Rights Amendment introduced in Congress was designated the "Lucretia Mott Amendment."[1]

Such a distinction would have had a mixed response from Lucretia had she been alive to receive it. On the one hand, she was spurred by her political and spiritual beliefs to respond publicly—so that vast numbers of people could hear her message and be called to the struggle. These "seen actions" were always important to Lucretia. But the quieter "unseen" actions, which helped preserve her inner congruity with her espoused beliefs, were even more important to her.

Active until her dying day, Lucretia was one of the first women in the United States to speak out publicly on social issues. Her achievements were many, each one remarkable because she never focused on consequences—but always on the integrity—of her actions.

Lucretia Mott, née Coffin, was born on January 3, 1793, on Nantucket Island, Massachusetts. Life on the island was essentially matriarchal. Since it was a fishing and whaling community, husbands and fathers were often away for six to nine months at a time. Mothers learned how to manage large families and run businesses; daughters learned to do the work that usually fell to sons. Women debated and decided community issues, such as how to fund public buildings and where to build them. The fact that men and women shared power and decision-making was not only a matter of practical necessity; it was a manifestation of Quaker doctrine, according to which men and women were equally capable and imbued with the same divine presence.

This strong Quaker community taught Lucretia the ethic of justice. The Quakers of Nantucket recorded their opposition to slavery in 1716, almost 150 years before the Civil War. Astonishingly ahead of their time, these Quakers believed that man-made hierarchies were oppressive to the human spirit, and they preached an egalitarian philosophy.

Quakers call themselves "Friends," and their congregations are called Friends meetings. There is minimal hierarchy in Quaker communities. Each individual has access to the divine with no need for an intermediary and can speak aloud as moved by the spirit. Quaker theology teaches that the Inward Light belongs to every person—every individual is special before God. Quakers trust this inner Light to guide them in interpreting the teachings of Christ and learning how to walk in the way of goodness and justice. Lucretia was taught to listen seriously to this inner voice and to trust it, and she did so for as long as she lived.

Lucretia's life became a testament of devotion to these inner teachings. Two teachings in particular were her beacons of right conduct: *do what you do in the spirit of love;* and *do not be seduced and distracted by worldly rewards.* In my mind, Lucretia embodied the possibility of living in such a way that every word, gesture, action, and reaction reflects the biblical commandment to *love thy neighbor as thyself.* For Lucretia, the goal was perfect congruity of the belief with the act, of the interior with the exterior. Rather than sermonize about this ethic, she lived it.

"Let Us Not Hesitate to Be the Messiahs
of Our Age"

Lucretia looked more like a conventional matron than the radical reformer she was. Inconspicuous and unremarkable in her appearance, she could easily have been overshadowed by the charismatic Sojourner Truth and eclipsed by the thundering orations of abolitionist William Lloyd Garrison. She was an unlikely coconspirator in the campaign to overthrow the established order, and her determination to speak the truth was formidable. Boldly, she raised the battle cry: "Let us not hesitate to be the messiahs of our age."[2] She was a social revolutionary packaged in Quaker codes and ethics.

She began her legacy of social protest early. In 1809, when she was just a teenager, Lucretia discovered that one of the male teachers at her Quaker boarding school was being paid 100 pounds a year while female teachers earned only 40 pounds. An innate activist, she didn't hesitate to complain and take action. While she didn't manage to achieve pay equity for female teachers, Lucretia had taken a stand. She referred to this incident as the defining moment in her life: "The injustice of this distinction was so apparent that I early resolved to claim for myself all that an impartial Creator has bestowed."[3]

In this single sentence, Lucretia illuminates the natural connection between faith and feminism:

- She believes in a Creator (Faith).
- The Creator is *impartial*—the Creator's gifts are meant

for *all* people equally, with no distinction or preference (Social Action).

• She feels entitled as a woman to claim the Creator's gifts, and further, she is *resolved* to do so (Feminism).

We can infer that her sense of justice comes from her understanding of what kind of Creator is bestowing the gifts of creation. In other words, her politics and her feminism stem from her faith in God-given equality.

In 1821, Lucretia was officially acknowledged within the Society of Friends as a minister, another noteworthy accomplishment for a woman. Quakers were one of the first religions to promote male and female leadership.[4] As an active member and minister, Lucretia began to challenge everything that did not conform to the moral principles that she believed reflected God's will for human society.

More so than any of the other women I write about in this book, Lucretia lived a life emulating the core concepts of Christianity. Whenever she saw injustice or pain, she was compelled to speak and act, guided by the Christ "who has come to teach his people himself."[5] Her actions and statements were neither eloquent nor complicated—they were as simple and direct as her love of humanity.

"An Ideal Marriage Union"

Lucretia met her future husband, James Mott, when she was a student at a Quaker boarding school where he was a teacher. A few years later, Lucretia became a teaching assistant at the school, and several of the teachers, including Lucretia and James, formed a group to study French. The French lessons only lasted six weeks, but Lucretia and James developed a bond that would last a lifetime. Within a few years, when Lucretia was eighteen, she and James married.[6]

They were opposite in many ways. She was short and dark; he was tall and blond. She was outgoing, cheerful, and impetuous; he was quiet, taciturn, and cautious. Yet these differences proved to complement each other. In fact, abolitionist William Lloyd Garrison called their relationship "an ideal marriage."[7]

After their marriage, the couple settled in Philadelphia, where James worked in a wholesale cotton business. James was as committed to justice as Lucretia, and when they learned that cotton manufacturers were slaveholders, they made a united moral decision to abandon the cotton trade and trade in wool instead, a change that brought substantial financial risk. The Mott home was an organizing hub for their joint and separate political activities. Not only were meetings frequently held there, but it was also used as part of the Underground Railroad.

Lucretia was an outspoken and unflinching leader, whereas James, though just as passionate, had a less strident approach. James's passion as an individual is seen in the reform work he conducted, independent of Lucretia. For instance, during the Irish potato famine of 1845–1847, he went to Ireland to assist other Quakers in famine relief efforts. James was incensed that so many were starving as a result of human injustice. He not only helped get food to hungry families, but also denounced the apathy of the British government and the world in general.

James and Lucretia had six children and a loving relationship. While most married couples at that time had separate beds, Lucretia and James were known for sharing a double bed all their lives. They frequently expressed their affection for each other, even in public. Lucretia and James missed each other, but they traveled individually when called on a mission. Lucretia and James manifested a *partnership* marriage in an age when it was unheard of. They divided household tasks and supported each other's work, emulating a model that is the envy of modern-day couples. Their marriage of equity came from their Quaker philosophy of justice. It is incredible to me that these two individuals created a near-perfect marriage out of their faith, and that this marriage addressed so many of the goals of modern feminism.

The couple seemed to integrate their political and personal lives with expertise and good humor. For instance, Lucretia concluded a long letter to Elizabeth Cady Stanton about education and professional opportunities for women with the words "Now I must go to darning old carpets." Lucretia maintained a flow between family and mission. Family members, especially her daughter Anna, usually accompanied her to her political meetings. Her colleagues in her work became dear friends. She would often bring homemade cakes to their organizing meetings. The value she gave to the power of relationship was fundamental to Lucretia's sense of social activism.

Lucretia's Political Journey

Abolitionist Activism

As a Quaker, Lucretia was trained to speak from the heart, needing neither a spiritual intermediary nor a political editor to be her mouthpiece. She felt duty-bound to condemn institutions that employed slaves or disallowed women. Her public image was not helped by her tendency to call herself a heretic.

Lucretia and James helped organize the American Anti-Slavery Society (AAS) in the early 1830s.[8] Although Lucretia had been present at all the meetings of the AAS and had actively participated in crafting its mission statement, she was not allowed to sign it because she was a woman. This propelled her to cofound the Philadelphia Female Anti-Slavery Society in 1833. She also helped convene the National Anti-Slavery Conventions of American Women, which met in 1837, 1838, and 1839.

In 1840, Lucretia and James sailed to London to attend the World Anti-Slavery Meeting. She was insulted when she was excluded from active participation in this international antislavery meeting. She had been elected as a voting delegate and had spent weeks crossing the ocean, but she was forced to sit in the balcony behind a screen, where she could see but not speak. We can imagine her outrage at being excluded in spite of seven years of sterling and outspoken leadership as a public organizer and speaker. She was able to transform her energy of fury into even greater passion for social reform.

"An Entire New Revelation of Womanhood" [9]

It was at the London meeting that Lucretia met Elizabeth Cady Stanton for the first time. While Lucretia was disliked by so many, she was respected and adored by her peers, including Susan B. Anthony and Elizabeth Cady Stanton. Indeed, Lucretia was one of the greatest inspirations and role models for Elizabeth—the two women became close friends. Elizabeth's many statements of love and praise for Lucretia give us insight into Lucretia's influence on one of our history's greatest reformers. Looking back at her first meeting with Lucretia, Elizabeth wrote:

> There are often periods in the lives of earnest, imaginative beings, when some new book or acquaintance comes to them like an added sun in the heavens, lighting the darkest recesses and chasing every shadow away. Thus came Lucretia Mott to me. . . . I often longed to meet some woman who had sufficient confidence in herself to frame and hold an opinion in the face of opposition, a woman who understood the deep significance of life to whom I could talk freely; my longings were answered at last. [10]

During the convention, Elizabeth and Lucretia were seated next to each other at a dinner party when several Baptist ministers started criticizing the women for trying to take leadership roles in the abolitionist movement. Elizabeth wrote:

Calmly and skillfully Mrs. Mott parried all their attacks, now by her quiet humor turning the laugh on them, and then by her earnestness and dignity silencing their ridicule and sneers. I shall never forget the look of recognition she gave me when she saw by my remarks that I fully comprehended the problem of women's rights and wrongs. How beautiful she looked to me that day.[11]

Elizabeth and Lucretia were inseparable throughout most of their time in London. Elizabeth writes about going with Lucretia and a group of people to the British Museum. On entering, they sat near the door to rest a few moments, telling the others to go on. Three hours later, they were still sitting there, too absorbed in conversation about theology and women's rights to see the exhibits in the museum.[12] The following day, Elizabeth went to hear Lucretia preach in a Unitarian church. Lucretia was the first woman Elizabeth ever heard speak in public. She wrote:

When at last I saw a woman rise up in the pulpit and preach as earnestly and impressively as Mrs. Mott always did, it seemed to me like the realization of an oft-repeated happy dream.[13]

Elizabeth also credits Lucretia with revealing to her our unquestionable right to freedom of thought, speech, and action: "When I first heard from the lips of Lucretia Mott that I had the same right to think for myself that Luther, Calvin, and John Knox had, and the same right to be guided by my own convictions . . . I felt at once a new-born sense of dignity and freedom."[14]

Elizabeth found it refreshing that Lucretia was "emancipated from all faith in man-made creeds, from all fear of his denunciations. Nothing was too sacred for her to question as to its rightfulness in principle and practice." When women were banned from the convention, Elizabeth asked Lucretia if she would rise up and speak anyway, if she felt called to speak by the Spirit. "Which would you obey? The Spirit or the convention?" asked Elizabeth. Lucretia promptly replied, "Where the Spirit of God is, there is Liberty."[15]

Feminism Is Born

Lucretia's visit to Seneca Falls, New York, in 1848 sparked the first Women's Rights Convention. Lucretia and Elizabeth were among the women who sat down to tea and rose up in revolution. The Seneca Falls Convention, organized by this group of five women, attracted more than three hundred women and approximately forty men. Elizabeth, Lucretia and several others wrote the Declaration of Sentiments and Resolutions, which is considered the founding text of the American women's rights movement. Based on the Declaration of Independence, the Declaration of Sentiments stated that, like men, women were born with certain natural rights. The document criticized men for denying women the right to vote, to hold property, to equal terms in a divorce, and to custody of children. It criticized men for blocking women's access to higher education and employment, and faulted the church for excluding women from the ministry.

The Declaration of Sentiments also built on ideas expressed at the First Anti-Slavery Convention of American Women, held in 1837. Years later, when Elizabeth was preparing to write the *History of Woman Suffrage*, Lucretia insisted that the start of the women's rights movement was at this 1837 convention, for this was where "the battle began." She reminded Elizabeth, who had not attended the convention, of the resolution from the 1837 convention that stated that "woman should move in the sphere Providence assigned her," transcending the limits of "corrupt custom & a perverted application of the Scriptures."[16] Elizabeth ultimately decided that while the 1837 convention deserved mention, she would not give it great significance in her history. Only recently are historians confirming Lucretia's assertion that the starting point for political organizing for racial and gender equality occurred at the spirit-filled, cross-racial, female-abolitionist meeting of 1837—truly where "the battle began."

Lucretia formed lifelong alliances with fellow reformers Elizabeth Cady Stanton and Susan B. Anthony. Elizabeth and Susan leaned on Lucretia for advice on their tactics, since of the three, Lucretia had the most experience and expertise. For instance, Lucretia urged Elizabeth and other women's rights activists to tone down some of their "fiery pronunciations" so as not to alienate the audience they were trying to win over. Elizabeth at first disagreed: "For [Susan B.] Anthony and myself, the English language had no words strong enough to express the indignation we felt at the prolonged injustice to women." However, they ultimately took Lucretia's advice: "We found . . . that, after expressing ourselves in the most vehement manner and thus in a measure giving our feelings an outlet, we were reconciled to issue the documents in milder terms."[17]

Lucretia became the first president of the post–Civil War organization founded by Elizabeth, the American Equal Rights Association. Through this effort, she fought to secure equal rights for women and blacks in all areas of life—not just suffrage. The first Equal Rights Amendment, named in her honor, was introduced in Congress in 1923 and finally passed Congress in 1972. But due to an insufficient number of states voting for ratification, it has still not been added to the Constitution. In the spirit of Lucretia, feminists regularly organize behind this issue, motivated by conviction, and determined in spite of repeated disappointment to win ratification of the Equal Rights Amendment. It's hard to believe that women still do not legally have equal rights.

Pacifism and Nonresistance

Like many Quakers, Lucretia and James were confirmed pacifists. They constantly clarified in public speeches and private conversations that pacifism did not mean being passive. In a stirring speech, Lucretia addressed this irony head-on:

I have no idea because I am a non-resister, of submitting tamely to injustice inflicted either on me or on the slave. . . . I am no advocate of passivity. Quakerism as I understand it does not mean quietism. The early Friends were agitators, disturbers of the peace. . . .[18]

Not only did they oppose war and violent resistance, they were adamantly against the death penalty. After the Civil War, Lucretia argued that slavery had been ended through "moral" rather than military warfare. Lucretia's voice would be a vital one in today's climate of compromised human security.

Balancing the Public and the Private

While Lucretia's public life was inspirational, I also want to discuss her private life: her quiet actions. I agree with Lucretia's ethic that private acts of integrity are the foundation of a more just and a more equitable society. She taught us that small moments of love in action can add up to potent agents of change. There are many stories of Lucretia's quiet activism such as when she collected food and clothing for black families in Philadelphia, and befriended Irish immigrants, helping them find jobs when they arrived during the potato famine.

Lucretia didn't feel comfortable paying minimum wages to other women to do what she considered to be her "dirty work." While she did hire domestic help, she paid them significantly higher than the norm, and she never allowed them to clean her bathroom or scrub her floors.

Lucretia and James became friends of William Lloyd Garrison, the great abolitionist. Lucretia was excited by Garrison's thundering passion and wanted others to hear him speak. She went to great lengths to organize a speaking engagement for him. When Garrison gave his speech, however, Lucretia was disappointed. Not only did he read his speech; he mumbled it. While most people would have been discreet,

Lucretia directly offered him this advice: "William, if thee expects to set forth thy cause by word of mouth, thee must lay aside thy paper and trust in the leading of the Spirit." Despite her criticism—or perhaps because of it—a lifelong friendship developed. And Garrison, heeding Lucretia's advice, became, in time, a powerful speaker.

This episode illustrates Lucretia's efforts to make sure that human rights messages were articulated clearly and strongly in the public realm—in many ways this is a part of Lucretia's "seen" or public work. However, embedded within the story is Lucretia's quiet effort to aid a comrade and friend in his own development; this is her love in action.

When I see aspects of Lucretia in myself and my loved ones, it gives me faith and hope. My daughter Kathryn had the opportunity to pursue postdoctoral studies at several esteemed universities abroad but chose instead to be near her grandfather, caring for him during the last year of his life. I saw Lucretia's spirit in Kathryn when she made this loving sacrifice with no regrets and only joy. This love in action, the commitment to right relationship and integrity, is essential to the success of any professed sociopolitical agenda.

Lucretia's life is one example of wholeness. I often think of her when I'm wondering about the balance in my own life. When I feel pulled in one direction or another—being a writer, a mother, an activist—I remind myself that Lucretia insisted on living in a balanced way that nurtured her own integrity.

Lucretia saw power in silence, spending time in silent contemplation and prayer was very important to her. Periods of silence helped ensure that she hadn't lost track of her deepest spiritual goals. Our son Josh has devoted himself to periods of silence as he participates in programs of meditation. As he has described the long periods of silence, I have thought about the long silences of the Quaker meetings Lucretia and James attended, a silence where one slows down to notice the little things. One day, Josh and I were taking a walk down a country road. I was lost in my conversation with him. But I noticed that he stopped to pick up trash on the side of the road, and he discarded it in a receptacle when we got to our destination. I would not have noticed the trash much less done anything about it. I was touched by Josh's gentleness and care. In this time of a fast-paced society, he takes the time to attend to the small things that, when accumulated, can make a large difference.

The Action of Lucretia Mott

Whether you are studying the beginnings of the women's movement, learning about antislavery societies, or reading about philanthropic efforts to ease the suffering of the poor, you will find Lucretia. She was everywhere on the political scene, formulating strategies, preaching transformation, writing letters, smoothing ruffled feelings, and nudging people toward better behavior. And her action also took the form of her commitment to prayer and Quaker practice. Her success in life seems to have sprung from a few simple convictions. Everything followed from these.

She believed that we are put on earth to follow the teachings of Jesus. We are steered by the Bible and by the divine voice that speaks to us when we wait quietly for guidance. Her theology was straightforward and her advice to the people around her was practical. She believed everyone had the opportunity and duty to be God's eyes, ears, and hands on earth.

The questions raised by Lucretia's life are "How are you called into action?" and "Are you faithful to that call?" Your actions might be public or so quiet they are never noticed, which Emily would have applauded. Your act of courage might be taking the time and developing the spirit to reconcile a relationship. Or it might be simply getting out of bed if you suffer from depression or going to that first A.A. meeting. You might be quietly writing letters to political prisoners through Amnesty International or sending an anonymous donation to help the orphans in South Africa. You might take time each week to go to the hospital nursery to rock the neglected babies with AIDS. You may have a strong desire to cultivate your own garden and participate in growing the food you eat, allowing time for your inner spirit to grow and be nurtured as well. You may be protecting and valuing time as a parent.

It is not important whether our actions are considered large or small; it is important that they stem from the center of our being. When we learn to live from our own authenticity, we activate our still inner voice. Although Lucretia was a lead singer on the world stage, she would have been perfectly happy singing backup for someone else—as long as the music was right and all the people were included in the dancing.

Chapter 7

DOROTHY DAY

1897–1980

Living Communion

I believe some people—lots of people—pray to the witness of their lives through the work they do, the friendships they have, the love they offer people and receive from people. Since when are words the only acceptable form of prayer?

—DOROTHY DAY

orothy Day *voluntarily* lived in shabby apartments, celibate but never alone, eating almost all of her meals in a soup kitchen, finding friendship in the company of crazy-talking people from the street. In her writings, she observes that relationship, when it is imbued with love, leads to abundant living. She describes a quality of relationship that transforms hardscrabble conditions and bleak surroundings into experiences that open the heart and give meaning to our lives. This quality of relationship is the achievement of communion—the coming into union with God, others, and ourselves.

One of the many ways Dorothy expressed her sense of communion was founding the Catholic Worker movement, a network of houses of hospitality for people who have fallen through the safety nets and are living on the edge of society. The Worker also published a newspaper, which sold for a penny. The paper analyzed the problems of capitalism, revealing the struggles of many workers and the unemployed. Her life was remarkable, not only because she overcame her own problems, but because she moved on to address the heart of the world's struggles. As a result of the lives she impacted, not only during her own lifetime, but in the years since, Dorothy is being considered for sainthood by the Catholic Church.

The Common Unity of Humanity

Dorothy's story is about transforming loneliness into communion with God. Ultimately, Dorothy's spiritual practice was relating on a daily basis to the divinity she believed resides in all people. Whether she was speaking to a prostitute, a bishop, or a potential funder, she honored all of them equally and with dignity.

Dorothy was born in Brooklyn in 1897, into a nominally Protestant family that rarely attended church. Yet, in her autobiography she recalls that by the age of eight she was deeply curious about religious people, and that by ten she attended Mass every Sunday. The next year, her father took a job in California, where the family relocated. After the 1906 San Francisco earthquake destroyed his offices, the whole family then moved to Chicago, where they remained for twelve years.

Such instability in these early years was hard on Dorothy. Throughout her life, she yearned for community. Once in Chicago, the family continued to struggle in isolation. Since her father was unemployed, they moved into a tenement apartment, exposing nine-year-old Dorothy to the shame and helplessness suffered by people with no economic base. When her father secured a job, the family moved to a more comfortable house in a middle-class neighborhood. Yet Dorothy could not shake the memories of Chicago's South Side. From that point on, she felt drawn to connecting with those who had fallen through the cracks.

Dorothy poured her thoughts into writing, utilizing her reading and research skills to search for answers. Her writing attracted notice and she won a scholarship to the University of Illinois. Two years into her studies she dropped out. But during those college years, she began a journalistic career that deepened her awareness of social conditions. Her interest in organized religion, which had been so keen when she was younger, waned to the point of being nonexistent because she felt that religion did nothing to improve the plight of the disenfranchised.

In 1916, she moved with her family to New York, where, at the age of eighteen, she joined the Socialist Party. She developed passionate political concerns on behalf of others, surrounding herself with artists and writers who were immersed in radical politics and protest. She advanced her career in journalism, publishing in left-wing papers such as the *New York Call* and *New Masses*. Her pain as a child had taken her into her dark shadow feelings, which she wrestled with for many years. Through her writing, she developed her voice and used it to call out for justice.

Dorothy was a young woman during the sexual revolution of the twenties. She saw women organizing to secure the right to vote. When they organized hunger strikes, she joined with them. Her solidarity with those she felt were being treated unfairly grew, and it wasn't long before she spent time in jail as a political protestor.[1] She wrote of a realization she had during her first experience in jail: "That I would be free after thirty days meant nothing to me. I would never be free again, never free when I knew that behind bars all over the world there were women and men, young girls and boys, suffering constraint, punishment, isolation and hardship for crimes of which all of us were guilty."[2]

In search of her path, Dorothy enrolled in a nursing program at King's County Hospital in Brooklyn. Working during the ravages of the influenza epidemic in 1918–1919, which caused the deaths of up to 30 million people worldwide, she encountered a bald woman on her ward who was loud, unruly, and rude. Everyone in the ward did all they could to avoid this woman's bed. One day, the woman began screaming for her wig. Seeing her upset, the nurses attempted to console her. The lady would not be mollified and bellowed,

"Love be damned! I want my wig." Dorothy stepped forward and insisted the woman be heard. She went through the patient's things until she found the old wig and simply put it on her without a word. The woman immediately quieted down. Reflecting on the incident later, Dorothy wrote: "She needed more than to be loved. She wanted to be respected."[3] This was a lesson Dorothy never forgot. Regardless of what she did from that day forward, she placed an emphasis on listening to every human being she encountered.

After a year in nursing, Dorothy returned to writing. At this point in her life, at the age of twenty, she became involved in an unhappy love affair with a fellow journalist. She became pregnant and had an abortion. Soon afterward, she married another man, but they were quickly divorced. Years later, she wrote an autobiographical novel, *The Eleventh Virgin*, which chronicled this dark period.

In 1924, she published her novel and used the proceeds from the sale of film rights to purchase a bungalow on Staten Island. At her bungalow, she entered into a common-law marriage with Forster Battingham, which lasted four years—the longest intimate friendship she had had. In 1926, Dorothy became pregnant. She felt overwhelming joy at the idea of giving birth to her child. She had begun to feel a stability that she had been longing for. In addition, she began to realize that something was missing from her radical political perspective. Surprising both herself and her comrades, she began to connect with the practices of the Roman Catholic Church. She had never been drawn to large institutions and had actually railed against them. However, the power she experienced in the love and prayer surrounding Catholic rituals spoke to her on a deep, intuitive level. She sensed that it was this philosophic and faith structure that had the best chance of addressing the needs of all humanity. She intuited the potential of a community attempting to live in faith. Writing about her gradual conversion, she attempted to articulate the mystery underlying the life she experienced around her:

> It is so hard to say how this delight in prayer grew on me. The year before, I was saying as I planted seeds in the garden, I *must* believe in these seeds, that they fall into the earth and grow into flowers and radishes and beans. It is a miracle to me because I do not understand it. Neither do naturalists understand it. The very fact that they use glib technical phrases does not make it any less of a miracle. A miracle we all accept. Then why not accept God's mysteries? I began to go to Mass on Sunday mornings.[4]

In the Catholic Church, Dorothy felt that at last she had found a global structure for pursuing a way to live together "on earth as it is in Heaven." For Dorothy, the Catholic Church became a large global family and taught a way to manifest living in "right relationship" with others. It was a place where people from every walk of life became unified. It was an organized ethic that, even if done poorly up to that time, had the potential for truly fostering communion.

But Dorothy paid a heavy price for her slow and steady immersion into a religious way of life. Forster, her partner, could not and would not tolerate her interest in religion. A fellow journalist, he had been an eager partner with her in her crusade for justice. As she intensified her engagement with Catholicism, however, he withdrew. Dorothy loved him and was yearning for a family. But she now saw religion and activism as being inextricably interwoven, and she could not abandon her growing faith. In fact, she wanted to convert to Catholicism. Their disagreements grew increasingly hurtful. Dorothy had wanted their daughter to be named Tamara Teresa, after Teresa of Ávila. When she also wanted her to be baptized a Catholic, her relationship with Forster shattered.

Dorothy agonized over this loss, but she could not abandon her growing faith. She began the next phase of her life as a convert and a single mother. Alone in New York City at the beginning of the Great Depression, she wrote:

> I was lonely, deadly lonely. And I was to find out then, as I found out so many times, over and over again, that women especially are social beings, who are not content with just husband and family, but must have a community, a group, an exchange with others. A child is not enough. A husband and children, no matter how busy one may be kept by them, are not enough. Young and old, even in the busiest years of our lives, we women especially are victims of the long loneliness.[5]

Dorothy understood broken relationships. Her accomplishments in holy living arose from her ability to transform brokenness into healing connection. She felt this mystery was achieved through her personal connection to both Jesus, the spirit-guided teacher, and Christ, the divinity. She took seriously the New Testament mandate to love the people who are hardest to love. She met Christ in the broken men and women who sought refuge and relief, and they met Christ in the sometimes cranky woman who sat down to listen to them. This newfound relationship with God transformed her relationships with others. Dorothy used love as a strategy, or perhaps as a weapon, as she forged relationships with everyone she met, wielding her belief that the divine resides in us all.

Her way of being religious was as nonconformist as her nonreligious life had been. She was skeptical about many of the practices of the institutional church. She preferred to trust in the personal relationship she had grown to experience with God. This relationship transformed her ability to be in community and enabled her to see the essence of those around her: "The longer I live, the more I see God at work in people who don't have the slightest interest in religion and never read the Bible and wouldn't know what to do if they were persuaded to go inside a church."[6]

For Dorothy, the bread broken at Mass wasn't any more holy than the bread broken at shelters and soup kitchens. Church didn't happen in a building. It happened in the way people related to each other. Christ wasn't any more present in the liturgy than he was when one person listened with compassion to the pain of another. Religion wasn't a set of ideas or dogma. Religion came to life in everyday connections to others. Because she had intimate experiences with brokenness, both in her personal life and in the lives of the community she served, her life was devoted to repairing ruptures among peoples of the world.

In 1932, in the midst of the Great Depression, she met Peter Maurin, an Americanized Frenchman who had long been associated with Catholic lay movements designed to recapture the spirit of poverty and service. He introduced her to a new Catholic consciousness movement that advocated the establishment of communal farms. With the support of Maurin, Day began to publish the *Catholic Worker.* Together, Maurin and Day created "houses of hospitality"[7] to provide basic food and shelter for people in crisis due to the Depression. The first house in Manhattan where she worked served eight hundred a day. The idea caught on and the houses began to proliferate.

The mission of this international lay movement is to acknowledge that our greatest calling as human beings is to fling open the doors of our hearts and to recognize we are all interrelated. Anything we do impacts the whole, and in affecting the whole, we are impacted deep within. In this way, relationship holds the power of the sacred.

In reality, however, many of us have trouble at times seeing the divinity of that problematic parent, our insensitive partner, or our rude neighbor. And while we can value our connection with those we respect, when someone we encounter comes wrapped in a repugnant and belligerent form, it takes practice to see their inherent divinity. Dorothy took seriously this ideal of communion with all; in fact, she took it literally. She said, "I always felt the common unity of our humanity; the longing of the human heart is for this communion."[8] Dorothy Day used the language of the "we" rather than the "I." She saw God in all of her relationships and therefore saw everyone and everything in union. Dorothy understood and lived the mystical life.

Dorothy was wary of those who came to the houses of hospitality to write articles, insisting "You should not write the things you do unless you mean them. In other words, do not write about hospitality unless you are willing to assume the obligations such writing brings with it."[9] And she recoiled at the suggestion that she was Lady Bountiful, handing out packages to those less fortunate. "I felt that charity was a word to choke over. Who wanted charity?"[10] Her vision was one of sacramental living, in which the giving of ourselves to others does not diminish, but enlarges and fulfills.

To experience this enlarged reality is to awaken to Life. If we are of God, then everything we do matters. We have a responsibility to manifest the divine—in matters great and small, when people are watching and when they're not. To wash the dishes can be a sacrament if we do it in the spirit of attention and love. Any of the tasks of our everyday lives can be done with thanksgiving and praise. To live in this way is to become pained when we hurt or are careless with others. I can type this paragraph in less than a minute, but it often takes a lifetime to learn to live its message.

There is a mysterious chemistry in authentic relationship. We are pulled, stretched, and humbled into our best selves. Many of us are in spurious relationships, pseudorelationships that are superficial, or less than honest. Authentic relationship is about honesty, openness, and respect of difference. The capacity to be in authentic relationship often breaks open our hearts. Dorothy believed that true prayer exists in the living of authentic, loving relationships.

The Catholic Church is now considering Dorothy Day for sainthood. I don't know whether she will become a saint, or whether she *should* become one, but I appreciate the fact that her life reveals some of the complexity of what "sainthood" is like. I have found in my study of these holy women that their lives are often fraught with broken hearts, despair, and chaos. I admire Dorothy, but I'm not tempted to over-romanticize her holiness. She wouldn't have either. To a journalist who called her a saint, she replied, "Don't call me a saint—I don't want to be dismissed that easily."[11]

When she was sixty-eight, Dorothy, a lifelong pacifist, traveled to Rome as a representative of the Catholic peace organization Pax Christi. The group requested that Vatican II issue a strong peace statement that include conscientious objection, Gospel nonviolence, and the banning of nuclear weapons.[12] Dorothy didn't just talk; she acted on her convictions in strategic ways.

When Dorothy was seventy-six years old, she met with Cesar Chavez. Chavez had formed the United Farm Workers of America, the first labor union in agricultural history to successfully organize migrant farmworkers.[13] Chavez and the United Farm Workers were gathering in California's San Joaquin Valley for a nonviolent demonstration against the Teamsters Union (IBT). Even at her age, Dorothy was arrested with other protestors and jailed for ten days.[14]

Dorothy continued to edit and contribute to the *Catholic Worker* for the rest of her life. She died in 1980, at the age of eighty-three. With an inherent understanding of the mystical power of relationship, she forged a connection with God that radiated broadly beyond her single life. Once she established the first house of hospitality, she lived the rest of her life amid the exuberant chaos of the masses. In addition to her autobiography, she wrote over a thousand articles and several books, including *House of Hospitality* and *On Pilgrimage: The Sixties*. Toward the end of her life, Dorothy said, "If I have accomplished anything in my life, it is because I wasn't embarrassed to talk about God."[15]

My daughter Leah and I visited the Catholic Worker offices several years ago to see how her work was being continued. I had a conversation with director Jane Sammon, who explained that she came to the Worker in 1972 and had spent the last nine years of Dorothy's life with her. She told me that what stood out for her was Dorothy's desire to live an outer life resonant with who she was inside, and to live in the spirit of Psalm 85, where "love and faithfulness meet together; righteousness and peace kiss each other." And that a year's subscription to the *Worker* is still only 75 cents. There were 120 houses when Dorothy was alive. And her spirit lives on in the 150 houses worldwide that exist today.

Living Communion

Dorothy's social activism created a revolution within the Catholic Church that mandated a relationship with the homeless and disenfranchised. Her life illustrates the way in which authentic, loving relationships happen. At some point, pain breaks our hearts open, exposing all of the need inside. It feels as though our life is about to end, but this is really where life begins. If we can surrender to the process, our narrow selves will begin to grow, the shallow places deepen, and we develop an expanded consciousness and a capacity for authentic love. Dorothy often quoted this Psalm: "Enlarge Thou my heart, O Lord, that Thou mayst enter in." This enlargement gives room for the spirit of God to take residence.

Dorothy's life is an example as we seek to experience living communion in our own lives. Are there places where you would like to feel more generous or less judgmental? Do you want to experience a deeper connection with those you love? A version of the golden rule to do unto others as you would have them do unto you is present in every major religion for a reason. Relationships are the place where the mystical experience can become alive. The phrase I remember reading as a child is still the beacon of my life: "The person who desires to see the living God face to face, does not seek God in the empty firmament of his mind, but in human love."[16] How we treat others is the single most important factor in determining our spiritual life.

Our relationships help us grow into our wholeness, into an undivided experience of self and other. Those we love mirror back to us disowned parts of ourselves by naming what is lacking in our lives. Our internal voice is strengthened as we cultivate our ear through listening to others. In this way, relationship is the thread that makes all the other themes discussed in this book possible.

Each of the holy women in this book, and each of you reading this book, is in relationship. And each relationship holds the potential for conducting the universal love of God. This is the secret behind the mystery expressed in I John 4:7: "Let us love one another, because love is from God; everyone who loves is born of God and knows God." Truly being in right relationship we find what the holy book calls "the abundant life."

Chapter 8

Weaving a Connection

Human beings are more alike than unalike, and what is
true anywhere is true everywhere.

—MAYA ANGELOU

In retelling the stories of these five spirited women, I haven't been concerned with dissecting the religious doctrine each woman espoused. I have focused instead on the *effects* her religious faith had in shaping her worldview and her sense of purpose. Seeing the dynamic of faith at work in these women's lives helps us understand its power. In this chapter, we will explore the possibilities of letting holy women guide us in the telling of our own stories. We all have a story to tell, many of us epic tales.

One Woman's Story Is All Women's Story

To what extent can we derive universal truths from the personal journeys of individuals? The microcosm and macrocosm mirror each other in nature. A snail shell is a spiral, as is the Milky Way. Why is that? By what design is this possible? Because we are connected by our common humanity, I believe that each of our individual lives is a microcosm of the whole. If this is true, then we have a useful way of gaining deeper insight into our current social problems and the resources to solve them. By seeing ourselves honestly, we have the capacity to understand others more deeply.

Choose any one person on this planet, regardless of nationality, economic status, race, religion, or gender. Speak with that person about their life—their hopes and dreams, their deepest fears—and you will have a hologram of the struggles we are all moving through as human beings. When we speak as a single person, we also speak for the collective.[1] Conversely, when we analyze any one social, political, psychological, or religious movement, we see how the processes of the many have application to each of us individually. It is striking that in whatever specific subject we immerse ourselves, be it biology or art history, the depth takes us to the breadth, and we attain a doctorate of philosophy.

Each holy woman in this book made specific decisions based on her individual feelings, but her decisions represent universal impulses. In this sense, her private life translated into political and cultural statements. Whatever form it took, her mission was to end separation and restore connection. She opened her arms and brought others into the experience of love and belonging. Her actions sent the message that no person is excluded from the human family and the love of God.[2] And we would not have known the lives of these women if they had not told their stories.

It was Maya Angelou who warned, "There is no agony like bearing an untold story inside of you." Are these parts of your story buried? Learn to tell your story, keeping in mind that our five holy sisters offer a template on how it can unfold. Think of the five stages as they have manifested in your own life, and consider the potential for healing at each successive stage. Emily's ability to express her Pain enables others to find a mirroring of their own grief and solace in the face of suffering. Teresa's writings on her spiritual journey have paved the way for countless others to take courage in the darkness of the Shadow. Sojourner's taking possession of her life, freeing and renaming herself, inspire those of us who seek to find our authentic Voice. In a world where most often "the end justifies the means," Lucretia's life of Action stems from the wisdom that the means are more important than the ends. Dorothy understood how every individual relationship holds the potential of a sacred union, of Communion. We are made collectively stronger by every woman who learns to embrace her story.

Telling Our Stories

A feminist is any woman who tells the truth about her life.

—Virginia Woolf

An important aspect of empowerment comes from sharing our stories with one another. And before encouraging you again to tell yours, I'll share some of mine. The structure I have given the lives of the women in this book has been helpful to me in understanding my own journey.

Just as we can see Emily, Teresa, Sojourner, Lucretia, and Dorothy as spirited women, we can see ourselves in the same light. The ways we are changing the world may not be so definite or so public, but we too are making the same heroic journey toward wholeness.

So in the pages ahead, I will chart out my journey. I tell my story with humility, since there is a part of me that hesitates to talk about myself in the same breath as I talk about the five women just discussed. However, it is my thesis that all of us belong in the same company, regardless of what we have or have not accomplished. These women's lives are a gift to us, indeed a call to live life to our greatest potential.

The point of telling our stories, even if only to ourselves, is to help us resurrect the parts we have buried. When we unearth them, even if it's difficult, we can integrate them into our sense of who we are. Often in our buried self our true power lies.

I believe that a meaningful way for women to construct their stories is in the company of other women. If you are reading this book as part of a group, so much the better. You might ask two or three of your number to share their stories during any given meeting. If you are telling your story for your private reflection, I hope you'll find meaning in the experience, as I did.

My Story

Stage 1: Accepting Pain

I was raised a southern belle in an environment where women were expected to please others, and as was customary, I developed those aspects of myself that others felt were appropriate. I had a lively imagination, much passion, and intense opinions about things, but I had trouble bringing all these aspects of my spirit to the surface. There were difficult parts of my family context that were never talked about and that felt overwhelming to me—things like my father's bigamy and my mother's unspoken pain, which I still find hard to talk about. I inherited a legacy of lies and betrayal that were never discussed, giving me little clarity about how to process them. I now see that while I was growing up, I had pushed down or disowned much of who I was. When Betty Friedan talked of the "feminine mystique" that buried hundreds of American women alive, she was talking about me. Through my teen years and into my twenties, I began to realize that until I reclaimed this disowned part and developed a full relationship with myself, I would continue to live only half a life. There were divisions inside of me that needed to be healed. My journey became a journey to find wholeness.

Though I was born into a family of wealth, I wasn't taught how to be in relationship with money. I am the second-youngest daughter of H. L. Hunt, the oil tycoon and the man who some said inspired the idea for the TV show *Dallas*. My mother, Ruth Ray Hunt, was a Southern Baptist who devoted herself to the blossoming of her four children and to her religious life. My parents came from humble if not downright poor beginnings. With only an eighth-grade education, my father won his first oil well in a poker game—a piece of good luck that became his route to financial wealth. In spite of the finery with which they surrounded themselves as adults, my parents raised their children with many of the simple traditions and values with which they themselves had been raised. It was these values and the love around me that became the foundation that allowed me and my siblings to transcend our difficult background.

As a teenager, I felt awkward about having more resources than my friends. Money is reflective of power in this society, and I coped with my discomfort by distancing myself from both money and power. I hid behind drop-waist flowered dresses and dutiful nods. When I visited my father's office in downtown Dallas or was with him as he was discussing the family business with others, I understood that I was supposed to listen with only half an ear.

My job as a woman within my family was to marry a savvy businessman who would manage my money. I dutifully married Randy, a delightful, high-energy law student who loved financial creativity, and I deferred all business-related tasks to him. The first year of our marriage, I taught in an all-black high school, and while I felt I was expressing some of my deepest values there, I couldn't find a way to sustain this experience. Soon I gave birth to two daughters and focused my attention on them. My other interest at the time was psychology. In retrospect, I can see that the study of psychology was the only way I knew to strengthen my own submerged voice. I was torn between my need to unleash my inner voice and my desire to please others by maintaining the cultural and familial role expected of me.

I tried to share with Randy what I valued about teaching those high school kids, and what I was learning through my master's degree studies in psychology, but he grew impatient with my interests. He wanted to share his passion for contributing to the wealth of the family oil business, but I couldn't listen. His interest in the business stirred the disowned part of myself that lay buried beneath my awkwardness about money. As my marriage splintered, I began to feel the many ways I was cut off from myself. Once I recognized this, it opened a door to the pain that I'd locked away. I realized how hurtful it had been to grow up in a "powerful" family while disowning my own inner power. After seven years of marriage, Randy and I divorced. Thirty years later, it is my good fortune that Randy is a dear friend to me and a devoted father to our two daughters, Kathryn and Kimberly. Looking back, it is clear that Randy and I were *both* playing roles that severed us from our authentic selves. Alienation from the self is as painful and tragic for men as it is for women.

Stage 2: Integrating Shadow

After my marriage failed, I knew I was in crisis and needed to take action. I moved to New York City with my two young daughters. I was sad to leave a remarkable, caring brother and two dynamic sisters that I loved very much. But in my state of crisis, I felt I needed distance. A divorced woman living with two young children was not a rare phenomenon in the

United States—but I felt very alone in a strange environment. Two tasks became essential for me. The first was to focus on taking care of my little girls, relishing the chance to simply enjoy them and be present with them in a way my mother had never been present for me. Second, I knew I had to develop a relationship with money if I was ever to become whole. Abdicating this part of my life was disowning part of myself. I found a stock investor willing to teach me what he knew, and I chose to invest in oil and gas companies as a way to learn about my family's business. While my family money had always felt like my father's, the profits I made from these investments felt like funds I could direct with a sense of greater connection.

Until this period of my life, I had not been a part of the women's movement. But I happened to read an interview with Gloria Steinem who said, "We can tell our values by looking at our checkbook stubs."[3] Knowing that I had more money than others, and since I wasn't interested in traditional venture capital, shopping malls, alma maters, or opera houses, I recognized how important it would be to learn to invest in what I considered most valuable: people. The statement "To whom much is given, much is required" seemed obvious to me. I had distanced myself from the faith of my childhood because of the hypocrisies I saw in the church; I felt its beliefs failed me. I dove into what I now feel was shadow work, and I grew to understand that I had the choice to either continue to analyze, blame, and critique the church (an easy but miserable way to live) or learn to live my life in such a way that the values I cared about could become manifest. Having assumed this as a goal, I now see how very hard it is to achieve.

I thought that since I had a poor connection to my own power, maybe I could best be of use by helping others who were disconnected from theirs. I felt a kinship with other women in New York who felt separated from crucial aspects of their lives or were disempowered. In low-income neighborhoods, women were advocating for a woman's voice on the City Council to represent their issues. Welfare mothers were banding together to start sewing projects and other microenterprises. Many women in churches and temples were barred from pulpits and decision-making circles, but they knew they had a call to ministry as well as the skills. Finding support from and for women became a deep passion that I now see came from my own struggle with my shadow side.

Stage 3: Finding Voice

It was the mid 1970s—I had never felt more alive and open to change, energized by the rediscovery and renewal of my self. My desire to learn how best to invest in people, especially women, led me to a simple but revolutionary model of philanthropy that was being created around the country— women's philanthropy.[4] I came upon an annual report of the Women's Foundation of San Francisco, and Tracy Gary, one of its founders, became an inspiration. Tracy encouraged women to pool their resources into women's funds around the country. Women's funds empower women everywhere.[5] Donors and community activists from diverse backgrounds sit side by side on boards, which raise and donate thousands and millions of dollars.

At the time that I discovered women's funds, they were only just beginning to proliferate, with thirteen scattered around the country. In 1985, I helped found the Dallas Women's Foundation, which became the fourteenth women's fund. Groups of women in other parts of the country were interested in starting funds and occasionally called me, asking if I would advise them. Over time, I realized that I could help create and fortify a national structure to support the growth of more funds. I had found a work to which I could bring my deepest self.

I became a member of the board of the Ms. Foundation for Women[6] and began to link with others in supporting strategic programming for women. Being on that board also offered me a forum for networking with other women, both personally and professionally. At our meetings, we had time to share our lives, and any topic was allowed: our struggle with financial debts, problems with our kids, our sex lives. Nothing was off limits *except for one topic:* if you wanted to talk about your reflection on some scripture or a recent prayer experience, a sudden hush would fall across the room. Faith and religion seemed to be taboo subjects.

Many feminists question how a "male" God could foster true equality. That's a good point. As I stated earlier, religion has been part of the patriarchy that reinforces women's second-class status. Historically, organized religion was a major obstacle to women who fought for the right to own property, vote, and earn equal pay. The glass ceilings in the corporate world didn't seem nearly as thick as those that forbade women to become priests. It was Marie Wilson, president of the Ms. Foundation, who captured a widely felt sentiment when she insisted: "I did not abandon the church. The church abandoned me." And it had.

Nonetheless, I was troubled by what I experienced as a deep split between faith and feminism, and I realized that it reflected a split within myself. Just as I had once needed to own my power and money in order to move into greater wholeness, I knew that I needed to integrate my faith into my daily life, and into my work, in order to express the fullness of my true self. I was going to have to find a way to use my own voice to make connections to women who were different from me and remember that for every difference there were countless commonalities.

Stage 4: Taking Action

Women's funds provided forums for women to explore issues of empowerment, money, and social justice. Within these forums I connected with a wide diversity of women who shared a common concern: the development of women's full potentials. I understood the frustration of community activists over the inadequate funds that traditional foundations allocated to women and children—those most impacted by the burden of poverty. And I empathized with the women of wealth giving major gifts to women's funds. Like me, they were questioning the way they'd been socialized to distance themselves from financial issues. Our gifts to these organizations were returned to us tenfold. In this way, and in so many

FAITH AND FEMINISM

more, my involvement with women's funds helped me connect with much of what remained disowned inside of me. I found a community of soul sisters, and the very money that had caused me such pain as a child became my way to heal the pain of others.

One day, I was called by a small group of women who wanted to start a New York Women's Foundation.[7] I knew I had to respond. This was my opportunity to give back to the city that had given me refuge when I was in crisis. The idea that New York City needed a women's fund was beyond doubt.

The privilege of cofounding the New York Women's Foundation was one of the defining moments of my life. I worked shoulder-to-shoulder with women who were diverse with regard to race, class, and sexual orientation but united in their commitment to support disenfranchised women in New York City. We were audacious in our fund-raising goals—and my voice was strong as I called everyone I knew in the country to make a donation.

There are now over one hundred women's funds in the U.S. and beyond. In the last ten years, programs strengthening the lives of women and girls, particularly low-income women and women of color. The New York Women's Foundation currently gives away $1 million a year. But one visionary woman rose up and pledged $100,000 for each of the next ten years. Two other women matched her million dollar pledge. This kind of action and the wielding of financial clout on behalf of women has never happened before in history.

Women, money, and faith—what would happen if these were brought together? In 1993, I founded a private foundation, The Sister Fund, named for my biological and soul sisters. Over the past decade, I worked with community organizers who joined the board, and together we have explored the meeting ground of spiritual vision and social activism. Deciding to be explicit about the nexus between faith and activism, our mission is to fund women's social, economic, political, and spiritual empowerment. For us, as for feminist theologians and the holy women in this book, faith finds its natural expression in action. While we know it is possible to work for justice without being religious, we believe that religious faith presupposes a mandate to write, speak, and act for social justice. Kanyere Eaton and Sunita Mehta lead, and exemplify the soul of, The Sister Fund.

I have watched a vast network of women helping women emerge from the first small impulses of organizing that began this movement—small but critical impulses not unlike that legendary tea party in Seneca Falls in 1848. Funds now exist in Mexico, Nepal, Amsterdam, Nicaragua, and South Africa. Clearly, women's philanthropy is an idea whose time has come.

Stage 5: Living in Communion

With women's voices growing stronger, they can join with men's to build healthy partnerships. When both voices are strong relationships can be more stable. I have always been in awe of the mystery and power of relationship. Where does love come from? What is its meaning? Relationship has catalyzed each new level of my spiritual development, and in this sense, relationship has always held sacred significance to me.

I was a teenager when I first read the work of Martin Buber.[8] His theory that relationship is a container for the spirit of God has had great meaning for me. In reading him, I crystallized for the first time my own thinking that when two people achieve a relationship of true mutual regard, in which the welfare of the other is as important as, if not greater than, one's own, something sacred is then born. Two people in right relationship become conductors of universal energy, of love. I am certain that Buber is right. I clung tenaciously to the idea that relationship can be a spiritual path, even through my years of painful divorce. One of the main motivators in my marrying Harville was his great passion to understand relationship.

During the years of our marriage, Harville and I have worked on developing and disseminating Imago Relationship Therapy. As is often the case, I was teaching what I most needed to learn. My deepest wounds and greatest strengths lie in my ability to see the potential for relationship in my life. Yet realizing the potential of relationship in our marriage was an arduous journey for us on a personal level. We struggled to manifest the Imago process. Like any system of values, it was easier in theory than in practice. We experienced one failure after another, despite the fact that the culture around us was applauding the work of Imago. We were acutely conscious that our own relationship was falling short of the ideals Imago embraced.

As we remained steadfast and committed to the process, the tension and struggle revealed to me some parallels between the work of Imago and that of empowering women. Imago Therapy teaches dialogue, which is touched on in the questions at the end of this book. This ever-deepening process enables people to grow skillful at articulating what they need and truly understanding what their partner needs. Imago Relationship therapy emphasizes the equality of two partners through the practice of dialogue and teaches them how to create an equal, intimate, and fulfilling bond.

How can any marriage exist between equals when women continue to have a subordinate status in society? This question illustrates how aligned my yearning for relationship was with my yearning for the full empowerment of women. Women and men can never be in right relationship with each other as long as women's voices are subordinated. Only by strengthening the voices of women is there a chance for true harmony and justice.

For a marriage to become healthy, the women's movement must succeed in the work of empowering women and liberating men from a false role of domination. A truly egalitarian marriage is a potent way to undermine the injustices of patriarchy, one couple at a time. For this to happen, women and men have to learn how to move beyond their socially prescribed roles and find their authentic human selves.

The theory that Harville and I worked to create became a beacon for us both, lighting the way as we moved deeper into the exploration and manifestation of an authentic relationship. It took hard years of struggle for us to move beyond roles and into our humanity. As Imago Theory teaches, those I love hold the key to unlocking the doors and showing me my disowned parts. Harville mirrors back to me the ways I need to be more focused. My children tell me I am indirect, and they challenge me to be more forthright and honest. Recently, one told me I don't seem to be remorseful when I make a mistake. With each mirroring back from someone I love, I continue on my path to wholeness, a never-ending journey.

Authentic connection carries the potential to heal what is broken in our world today. Learning to be in authentic connection occurs two by two. Marriage is certainly one place for such a revolution, yet *all* our relationships hold the potential for this healing to varying degrees. While I saw the potential for Imago as a therapeutic practice, I knew it would only be possible if two things occurred: first, women had to be empowered to take part as equals in the relationship; and second, there needed to be an understanding that the achievement of empathy between two people invites the spirit of God to be born anew in the world. To me, relationship is sacred because the spirit of God is manifest in empathic connection.

I hope my story helps you see how I have been encouraged in self-examination by the examples of others. Please add your voice to mine so that the women's movement can integrate all of our strength and stories. The real question of empowerment is intimately connected with our capacity to be in relationship with others and with ourselves. This is the underlying work we all have to do on the path to wholeness.

Toward Wholeness

My intention in this book has been twofold: to help secular feminists begin to trust the possibility that faith can lead people to effective activism, and to encourage religious women and men to consider feminism as essential to the divine plan for love and justice.

Bringing the five spirited women of this book into our lives has highlighted for me the artificiality of trying to keep feminism and spirituality separate. It's time to heal the rift. Why not become serious about a dialogue whose purpose would be to nurture mutual understanding and respect for differing views? Why not engage in a dialogue that acknowledges the importance of bringing *all of what we are* to discussions about the social issues? I know that the thoughts I've expressed here are only part of the dialogue. Let's *all* join the discussion about how we can best work together in a sustained and effective effort for social justice.

We will need to seek new ways of connecting with each other. If we were given the mandate to seek as many alliances as possible, we would see our differences and disagreements in a new light. Differences would become potential points for a new connection. We would become more attentive to developing the language of dialogue and would become more whole in the process. This is the only work that can save us, the only work worth doing.

Afterword

Toward a Whole Feminism

This is no simple reform. It really is a revolution. Sex and race, because they are easy and visible differences, have been the primary ways of organizing human beings into superior and inferior groups . . . We are talking about a society in which there will be no roles other than those chosen or those earned. We are really talking about humanism.

—GLORIA STEINEM

G loria *always reminds us* of what is important. Yes, we want reform, but what we are truly about is revolution. It will take several revolutions of consciousness fueled by both faith and feminism to achieve our desired state of humanity. I have told the stories of five holy women who knew the importance of introspection that leads to integrous action. They have left us a legacy of hope, stemming from the deep recesses of their faith. Now we will gather up some of the lessons from these pages and weave them together into a strategy for a more integrated future. I will begin with a comment about the wholeness of religion and then move on to the purpose of this Afterword, which is the wholeness of feminism.

Beginning with the *Women's Bible* edited by Elizabeth Cady Stanton, but in a much more focused way the last three decades, women have asserted their own voice in the theological realm. Women have advocated for a place within academe to become feminist theologians and scholars, and revisionist historians who resurrect women's contributions to religious history. As a result, valuable evidence of women's contributions to religious tradition have been unearthed. Feminist theologians are lobbying for a theology that has the same goals as secular feminism: justice and dignity for all.

Feminist theologians over the past few decades have produced magnificent scholarship about women in the Bible, particularly the women who surrounded Abraham, Moses, Paul, and Jesus. Paul's colleague Phoebe, for example, was a deacon who had the power and financial independence to fund Paul's travels. Patriarchal interpretations of history did a disservice to Phoebe by calling her a servant instead of a deacon, and feminist theologians are retelling her story. Historians are resurrecting the importance of house churches as the earliest places of Christian worship. Scholar Bernadette J. Brooten has won a MacArthur fellowship for her study of house churches and women's roles in early Christianity. As long as worship took place within the private realm of the home, women were ministers, equal in partnership with men.

Afterword: Toward a Whole Feminism

Only when churches outgrew homes and became public institutions did the role of men become dominant. But just as they did centuries ago, women are once again rising in the clergy, insisting on sharing offices, leadership, and scholarship, or as Elizabeth Cady Stanton would say, "overcoming the monopoly of the pulpit."[1]

There is a renewed interest in the role of Mary in the Godhead, with many asserting that the sacred feminine presence must be realized in order for Christianity to gain its wholeness.[2] A large grassroots movement around the world reclaimed the importance of Mary, even while she had been diminished by church hierarchy. Simultaneously, Jewish feminist theologians have been writing about Sarah and Miriam, just as Muslim feminist theologians have been writing about Khadija as a businesswoman and spiritual advisor to the prophet Mohammed, and Aisha as military leader.

Andal and Mirabai were Hindu women saints and leaders of the devotional Bhakti movement that initiated the religious liberation of women. Women such as Janice Dean Willis and Ven. Karma Lekshe Tsomo are contemporary "scholar-practitioners" of Buddhism who are telling the stories of the female sides of Buddhism as well as teaching about the faith. Contemporary Muslim feminists such as Nobel Peace Prize–winner Shirin Ebadi insist that their Prophet cared about women's rights, and their message has profound social and political implications the world is crying for. In all faiths, there has been a rise of the feminine that speaks to the need of women to see their faith reflected in their God.

A Model of Wholeness for Feminism

Insofar as the women's human rights movement is only secular, and not also owned by religious women who share its values, the battle to defend the rights of all women is weakened.

—CHARLOTTE BUNCH, Executive Director,
Center for Women's Global Leadership

Those of us who work in the women's movement care about it deeply. We have worked alongside each other, battling against patriarchal structures and helping to elevate women's status. We are pleased with what we have accomplished and yet our work is far from completed.

We need to preserve the movement's radical perspective so that it remains cutting-edge as a powerful political force. We must also increase the number of women who feel included. When we fracture our potential for united action and divide ourselves along social, political, economic, or religious lines, we diminish our power. We lose the opportunity to work uniquely as women in relationship. In fact, we do no better than those who stay within the patriarchal model of separation and competition. The more we can grow in coalition, widening our circle of relationships, the stronger we will become. To me, this especially includes recognizing and integrating women of faith. After all, the women's movement is a living, evolving organism. Like all living things, it is a dynamic system rather than an inert entity. Its capacity for cooperative and creative responses to changing circumstances is what has kept it alive.

This observation that the women's movement has the same kind of living dynamism that other organisms have, combined with my propensity to see the individual mirrored in the whole, has brought me to an unexpected conclusion. I think that the five stages of growth that characterize an individual woman in her journey are relevant to feminism as a social movement. *What if we applied the stages of challenge and growth that we've observed in holy women to the feminist movement as a whole?* Doing so would allow us to understand the religious-secular split within the movement in a deeper way. Here, briefly, is the thesis:

- **Pain.** The women's movement was born from the struggle and pain of women who for centuries were kept from their full humanity. Women's contributions to history were ignored. Their fractured, broken lives, and muted voices have been the price of an oppressive patriarchy. Our ability to evolve and embrace new circumstances while remaining true to our relational and spiritual roots will help usher us forward into the future.

- **Shadow.** From the beginning, the ideal was that feminism would be a movement for *all* women, so that a diversity of perspectives would be represented. As time went on, though, it has been hard to maintain this ideal. We have to ask whether feminism is currently a place where the many faces of the feminine can find a home. Women of faith have often been excluded, and acknowledgment is rarely made to the religious roots of feminism.

• **Voice.** Women began to speak out about the need for revolutionary change. They began to tell their own stories and to cry out against abuse and injustice, as well as voicing the potential of an enlightened society. In being heard and hearing, voices gained clarity and prepared the way for action.

• **Action.** Women broke down the barriers that deprived them of education, took their seats in boardrooms, and marched up the steps of Capitol Hill. We have made progress securing health care, providing increased educational opportunities, investigating better hiring and promotion practices in corporate settings, and influencing legislation aimed at equality of opportunity. Thanks to women's powerful actions, the status of women has advanced undeniably all over the world during the last 150 years.

• **Communion.** This is where we are headed. We are pointed toward the realization that we are all interconnected, and that the sacred resides in our connection. We have, as a movement, articulated and spoken our vision for a more egalitarian world. As we share our own hard-won voices with the world, we achieve a state of consciousness of a deep, living regard for one another, and we move into communion.

Afterword: Toward a Whole Feminism

As we review all we have accomplished, it's clear that we have not yet achieved this last stage of transformed relationships with others. Why? Because feminism has not yet integrated its Shadow, those elements of suffering and struggle necessary to realize the spiritual. I suggest that a *disowned spirituality is a shadow of the feminist movement.* The movement has kept itself from full development by denying, ignoring, and rejecting parts of itself, including its spiritual legacy. I have come to see that a major part of the shadow of the women's movement is the spiritual, faith-based dimension that was present early in the movement's history.

I don't mean this to sound like a criticism of the women's movement, which I embrace as family. I trust that self-criticism is a healthy part of movement building. The movement did exactly what it needed to do when we needed it most. When the movement was in its early stages, it was fragile and under intense attack. Feminists needed to stand united for equal rights in the workplace, even though this position alienated women who chose to stay home and raise their children. The movement also needed to stand united in opposition to the oppression and patriarchy of the church, even though this focus left religious women standing outside. Ultimately, the movement gave women across the country permission to claim basic and inherent human rights for themselves. But with each step of progress, there was intense societal backlash and certain groups felt left outside.

But feminism is organic and will ultimately invite back those for whom God is experienced daily and who value their spiritual perspective. Many of the women I spoke with in Beijing talked about the detrimental effects of the rigid attitudes of both feminism and religion that keep the two separate. If we do not confront the barriers that prevent the integration of feminism and religion, we will not move beyond them.

Integrating Our Shadow

My soul cries out "Holy!" I embody a driving, burning, inner discernment that must be acted out before neighbor, community and the Creator.

—REV. AUBRA LOVE, Executive Director, Black Church and
Domestic Violence Institute

Just as Teresa of Ávila worked to integrate her Shadow, so must the women's movement. As I have indicated throughout this book, I believe that this means making room for the power of faith. There are many reasons that the wedding of faith to feminism is important, in fact crucial. I offer the following:

1. We would broaden the women's movement to include many justice-seeking women and men in our own society, including those who work out of their faith tradition. Innumerable women from diverse cultures who do not separate their faith from their feminism would feel more welcome. We would reveal to others the relevance of faith language for our social justice mission, rather than abdicating this language to those who would oppose equality and justice. We would speak with pride of the women's liberation movement as a

movement to liberate the spirit, as a spiritual movement to help unify and nurture us all.

2. We would invite a reliance on something bigger than ourselves, on the energy of the sacred. This reliance would symbolize our willingness to open ourselves beyond the Western view that prizes the individual. This is hard for Westerners trained in self-reliance and autonomy. But such largesse would help us make the leap of trust in each other, and to the sacred energies beyond.

3. We would reflect and draw on the faith traditions of our parents and grandparents. When we sever ourselves from our tradition, we cut ourselves off from what is vital and living in our souls. G. K. Chesterton, journalist and poet, said, "Tradition means giving a vote to the most obscure of all classes, our ancestors. It is the democracy of the dead." His words are echoed with poetry and spirit by former Sister Fund board member and Native American community organizer Pati Martinson:

> What sustains my work on a very personal level is that I know that my ancestors dreamed me into existence. I've lived to see my grandchildren, and I often dream of their grandchildren. As I do my work, I always have this sense that, not just within my family, but within the family of human beings, I can see future generations in the eyes of infants, as well as in the eyes of elders.
>
> (Pati Martinson, Co-Director of Taos County Economic Development Corporation, The Sister Fund Special Report)

To ignore our tradition is to reject the prayers and wishes that our mothers and grandmothers held in their hearts for us. Given the religious roots of American feminism, an inclusion of women of faith would allow the women's movement to be reconnected to its own history, culture, and tradition.

4. We would, through our faith practices, become more rooted and connected to a consciousness larger than our own. Religion and faith in the divine fortify and sustain many of us in the struggle. Many Western feminist activists have said to me that after working a lifetime, marching and lobbying, they have found themselves spiritually bereft. The five activists in this book, as well as revolutionaries from Harriet Tubman to Gandhi and Martin Luther King, were sustained and fueled by their faith. Weaving together our faith and feminism would shift our activism away from fear and anger, and toward the unifying power of love.

When we fully re-member, our diversity can be our greatest strength. Women must see themselves mirrored in motherhood, in homemaking, in public service, in business, in academia, in artistic expression, and yes, in the divine. We will applaud feminists who are courageous enough to publicly take on controversial issues and risk being attacked for their insistence on truth-telling and justice. We will also embrace those women engaged in a quieter work, painstakingly ensuring that the exterior reflects the interior. I maintain that every woman committed to truth and justice is a holy woman and a hero no matter how quiet and private her life and work.

If I were to weave the issues and questions raised in these

pages into one message, it would be: **Faith and feminism need one another to complete and fulfill the highest potentials of their respective missions.** They are essential to each other's goals. Feminism can prevent religion from becoming so closely identified with the patriarchal. Religion can prevent feminism from becoming parochial and isolated. It is time to remember the religious roots of American feminism and reincorporate those elements that have been left out. Feminism needs to be open to the variety of religious experience.[3]

The Journey to Wholeness

What would such a relational and inclusive feminism look like? For feminism to move toward wholeness, we will need to shift from configuring in polar opposites and move toward convergence across vast differences of thought and method. I offer four signposts to guide us on this difficult but strengthening journey. Each signpost is a pair of polarities, which we can blend within ourselves and within our movement in order to move forward.

May we shed any illusion of having all the answers, and rather, open ourselves up to new experiences, ideas, and relationships. In brief, we must value:

- Listening as much as Speaking
- The Local as much as the Global
- Money as much as Mission
- The Collective as much as the Individual

I develop these four ideas below as our potential areas of growth.

1. Listening and Speaking

As feminists, we have made great strides in the *speaking* part of this dialogue process. Like Sojourner Truth, many of us have found our voice. Now we need to practice the other part of the process, which is *listening*. It is time to strengthen our ties to other sectors of the culture by cultivating the kind of listening that searches for common ground. That means learning to listen from the heart as well as the head. In some meetings at the Beijing conference, Western women were asked to speak only after three women from the global South had spoken. I don't think we could go wrong if each of us took the pledge to speak 50 percent less and listen 50 percent more. We will be along the road to *hearing each other into speech*. Listening, then, is the key to ending the split between faith and feminism.

To the religious woman who does not feel included or reflected in feminism, and to the feminist who feels uncomfortable with religion, I will say the following: My faith is the single reason I have devoted my life to social justice. It is faith that brings me into relationship with my entire human family. Women around the world, fighting for justice against all odds and often at risk to their lives, are all holy women to me. I want to listen to their stories every chance I get.

What is it like to be a welfare mom? A lesbian wanting to raise a child? An incarcerated mother? A woman of wealth struggling with guilt? A man doing the best he can to keep his family together, who is accused of being domineering? In our efforts to prescribe solutions for world problems, do we take the time to ask questions like these and then to quietly listen to the answers?

I believe that our work for equality and justice will be deepened if we pause to check in with our brothers on earth. What if we were to say to men: *How are you doing? Do you appreciate the women's movement or has it made you feel threatened? Do you ever feel there is a role that society expected for you to have no needs of your own and to be devoid of emotion? Is there something you are longing for?*

The spirit of connection is captured for me through the Imago dialogue process, where the focus is on the development of deep listening through the mirroring, validating, and empathizing of one another. We know that dialogue does not happen because two people are talking but because two people are *listening*. What if this unparalleled act of listening were the hallmark of the women's movement? Transformed relationships lead inevitably to transformed social institutions. This *listening* movement would focus on a policy of love in action and put individual spiritual experience in the service of that goal.

2. *The Local and the Global*

As a white American woman of wealth, I am acutely aware that the decisions and actions of the world's wealthy create devastating conditions in poverty-stricken communities around the world. My friend and colleague Rev. Linda Tarry-Chard is an African-American ordained minister who served on the founding board of The Sister Fund. She has devoted the last decade of her life to bringing economic justice to black women in South Africa, and she has taught me much about the devastating conditions in that part of the world. My daughter Leah was able to travel to South Africa last summer and intern for Linda's organization, Project People Foundation.

Recently, Linda told me that not a day goes by without her mother and her talking. I told Linda that this idea made me feel painfully deprived, as no white woman I knew, and certainly no wealthy white woman, talked with her mother daily. I decided to call Leah and ask her if we could quietly revolt against a culture that fosters a forced independence between mothers and daughters, and she was more than willing. Leah and I do our best to talk daily. This connection fills me with hope. The culture of dissociation in which I was raised is gradually being transformed, and I am healed as I and we grow in connection.

Linda helped bring into my life an ethic shared by many third world women and their daughters. Also, I mentioned earlier that women in other parts of the world tend to be less segmented about their faith and feminism. In fact, I have found women from other countries to be less segmented in general. In our culture, we have compartmentalized ourselves to the point that we are less effective; for example, even in our counseling community rape counselors rarely talk with domestic violence counselors. This lack of communication compromises our service to women. There is a lot for us to learn. I have had the privilege of working with courageous feminists from Africa, Asia, and Latin America, and almost all of them share:

- A hopeful outlook rather than a pessimistic, angry one

- A rootedness in points of convergence rather than points of conflict and opposition

- An evolved understanding of global issues and the ability to connect their own issues to others

- Knowledge of several foreign languages, which helps connection across difference

- An interest and expertise in making limited resources stretch as far as possible

- A willingness and openness to involve men in the work

I notice that instead of listening to our sisters from the global South, we have a tendency to preach to and infantilize them. The necessity to separate and categorize our thoughts and experiences tends to be a Western one. In Western thought, something is either true or false. And part of the problem is that we are arrogant enough to believe that we can *know* anything. If we rid ourselves of the illusion of certainty, and admit that there are things we don't know, we will become more open to perspectives different from our own. I suggest that we open ourselves to the excluded middle, the *maybe*, the humility, and the uncertainty—the gray between the black and the white. The admission "I don't know," generally leads to a question such as "What do *you* think?" and before you know it, a new connection has been made.

American feminism, with its dedication to sociopolitical issues, seems to have forgotten the human need for beauty, love, and joy—we have forgotten women's spirits. The women of Afghanistan stunned the world by rising up against the brutal religious extremism of the Taliban. They not only held underground schools because they believed that education is a birthright for both boys and girls, they also risked their lives to run underground beauty salons and musical gatherings because their feminism reinforces their belief that beauty and joy are as essential as education.

Through the work of The Sister Fund, I have been witness to some of the stellar organizing being done by feminist leaders in Afghanistan after the fall of the Taliban. I watched with admiration as Sunita Mehta birthed and nurtured a grassroots organization, Women for Afghan Women, within the offices of The Sister Fund. Sunita often refers to her group as "small in size but huge in vision and dreams," prioritizing the ethic of connection and diversity over all other aims and goals, and refusing to sever the religious from the secular, Muslims from non-Muslim, feminism from Islam, and the local from the global—the work of Women for Afghan Women bridges the reality of Afghan women in Queens, NY, with that of their sisters in Kabul and Kandahar.

We must heal the current schism between those feminists working on a local level and those working on international women's issues. Local voices render international human rights activism authentic and relevant just as international voices deepen and broaden community-based activism.

3. *Mission and Money*

I grew up with grace and hope at the core of my faith experience. Grace, shared through the unconditional love of God and family, allowed me the possibility to be all that I could be. Hope, arising from my life-long journey with Christ, made the building of community a passion. This combination of experiencing freedom borne out of grace and understanding hope as a verb, made a life of activism essential.

—CHRISTINE GRUMM, Executive Director, Women's Funding Network

Christine Grumm's "hope as a verb" is expressed through her work to strengthen women's funds around the world. Economic justice is a high priority on the feminist agenda. While economic disparity is the largest obstacle to economic justice, the lack of contact and trust between the wealthy and the poor is also demoralizing. My tenure on the New York Women's Foundation board taught me that you don't have to be rich to make a donation, and you don't have to be poor to receive one. Great friendships across the socio-economic spectrum were forged on women's foundations boards when we felt united in our mission.

Women raising serious money for their mission is a historic first. I came across words of Matilda Joslyn Gage that put the success of women's funds in perspective. Gage was a nineteenth-century activist who stood shoulder to shoulder with Elizabeth Cady Stanton and Susan B. Anthony. In the late 1880s, these three women co-authored a six-volume history of women's suffrage. At one point, as she reflected on the impressive growth of women's rights and suffrage associations, Gage bemoaned the fact that most of the work was being funded by men:

> With the exception of $1,000 from Lydia Maria Child, we have yet to hear of a woman of wealth who has left anything for the enfranchisement of her sex. Almost every daily paper heralds the fact of some large bequest to colleges, churches, and charities by rich women, but it is proverbial that they never remember the women's suffrage movement that underlies in importance all others. . . . Is it not strange that women of wealth are constantly giving large sums of money to endow professorships in [men's] colleges yet give no thought to their own sex—crushed in ignorance, poverty, and prostitution . . . ?

Why are we so ready and eager to pledge our wills and determination to women's issues but feel such a block when it comes to raising funds? If we are committed to feminism, we must be equally committed to securing the money for our mission.

My daughter Kimberly is an example of uniting money for a mission to help the landless poor in Central America. She is an activist for the housing and economic justice organization, the Agros Foundation.[4] With the money she raises, the farmers rent and work the land from Agros that they eventually purchase outright. The Agros staff prays for the farmers as they and their families regain control of their destinies.

Our challenge, as we work toward justice, is to grow both our money and our mission, making sure both are in alignment. If we stay committed, the results will be a world where women have a greater chance to prosper.

4. *The "I" and the "We"*

For me, justice is relational: it's about being in good relationship with everything that there is . . . In my understanding, a web of awareness and consciousness connects us, and the boundaries between our different forms are permeable. (Mary Churchill, Cherokee, Professor of Women's Studies, University of Colorado at Boulder)

The concept of the "we" is one of the cornerstone principles of the Native American faith. Whereas an integrated, whole feminism is a guiding value for the future, it is also a remembering of the evolved consciousness of the people who lived on this continent before European people came here and systematically destroyed their society. The ties that bind feminist vision with Native American principles are apparent. For instance, on her way to the famous tea party and the Seneca Falls Convention, Lucretia Mott had visited the Seneca Indians. Both Mott and Matilda Joslyn Gage developed a sense of justice influenced by the more relational and gender-balanced culture of native tribes. As these two women led in forging the new feminist vision, they drew from their appreciation of native cultures and traditions.[5]

Feminism has always operated from a strong ethical base of values. On this base, I see us building a movement that includes the *spiritual values* of relationship, as well as the willingness to recognize and overcome differences.

Feminism has been defined as activists working against oppression. It includes all women working for the right to fulfill their unique potential. Women and men can choose to be CEOs, stay-at-home parents, nuns or monks, ministers, entrepreneurs, or activists. No one choice is valued over another. But we hold high the ethic of our interconnection, that we are all part of the "we."

I see glimmers of this vision in the work of my daughter Mara. Mara is a testament to this ethic of connection, seeing the oneness of the earth and the sea, and our dependence on it all. She is a board member of RisingLeaf Watershed Arts,[6] an organization in California that promotes ecological awareness through the arts. For Mara, "we" is a oneness with all species—both large and small. Her consuming concern is for the dying sea, now 25 percent polluted from human waste and over-fishing. Mara is growing a consciousness of the "we" that we all must develop if our planet is to survive.

I once heard someone say that the women's movement has lost its capacity to dream. If that is true, we must spark our imaginations again and envision a compelling future for ourselves. The women's movement is essential to help the world usher in the next great agenda—social equality. Feminism is a counter and a balance to our political system, which is corrupted by self-serving involvements that make it ineffective. What if people knew that feminism could be trusted to help find solutions that are inclusive and guided by the spiritual values we have discussed?

Like Gloria Steinem, I am calling for revolution, not reform. Feminism is helping to usher in a paradigmatic shift of consciousness from the individual to the collective. My friend and co-founder of the New York Women's Foundation Anne Mendel reminded me once that the key question within feminism has changed from "Do we agree on the party line?" to "Where are the points of connection—can we find a way to be in relationship with each other?" The Newtonian physics of isolation and separation has made way for quantum physics, which theorizes that nothing can ever be isolated.

We cannot do this hard work of reform unless we recognize how interrelated we all are with each other and the sacred energies around us. Within our society, we emphasize the individual and their rights. However, individuals are shaped in relationship. It's time to reform our sense of independence. Relationship must become the definitive culture of feminism. If we can develop the inner strength to connect to our own disowned selves, we will be ready to connect to each other, and "the other." Moving past the "us and them" mindset will lead to improved relationships. We need the courage to move beyond the boundaries.

My son Hunter is a freshman at Columbia University, and I was thrilled to learn that he is one of only two men in the college's leading women's organization, Productive Outreach for Women. The New Testament, to me, is a message of love and human rights, and there is no doubt in my mind that Jesus would sign on and pull up a chair right next to Hunter. At its roots, Christianity was not ruptured along the seam of gender; like feminism, it embraces our innate connection.

This vision of feminism is a tall order. Are we up to the challenge? You now know from reading these words that I think we are.

We must keep in mind the women's movement is like an endangered species. We must be vigilant, large in number, and gloriously diverse if we are to protect our vision of justice for all. Patriarchal forces are very much alive in our world and are actively engaged in eroding women's hard-won rights everywhere. They are particularly apparent in right-wing political forces and extremist trends within most world religions. Let us stay true to our mission and keep our faith defined in a loving and inclusive way. Since the Beijing conference was a galvanizing moment for many of us on the road to a whole feminism, let us make a pact that we use Beijing Plus Ten, which will be upon us in 2005, as another opportunity for us to connect, both physically and in spirit, to each other. Let *relationship* be our new mantra, our new slogan, our new consciousness.

We Are Not Alone

Let's suspend the constraints of space and time for a moment and imagine a Gathering of Spirited Women. Our guest list would include the women we've already met—Emily Dickinson, Teresa of Ávila, Sojourner Truth, Lucretia Mott, and Dorothy Day. Present also would be other outstanding historical women, such as Joan of Arc, Harriet Tubman, and Catherine of Siena. Mixed among them would be women that you and I know personally. And of course you and I would be there too. Can you imagine the scene? There would be laughter and warmth. Some quiet conversation and even noisy confrontation. We imagine color, movement, intensity, and passion! The surprise might be how few of us look heroic or brave. I'm not sure we know what the heroic feminine looks like, but we do certainly have a sense of what this gathering would sound like! The scriptures say that when two or three who care about the transcendent are together, God is there in the midst. There is no doubt that we would be sustained by the sacred energy in the room and that we would feel encouraged and supported as we go out into the world to follow our own calling.

If we were present at such a stellar gathering, listening in on the conversation, what would we learn from the courageous and spirit-driven social activism? Most of the guests would be from a different world than our own. Would they have anything concrete to offer us, as we struggle to understand what we should be doing to make the world a better place?

The world we struggle to understand is more complex, more diverse, and more ambiguous than it has been in the past. We are now isolated within a mass culture. In the West we are materially rich but often spiritually impoverished. We live within a global, interdependent economy yet, at the same time, we build ever-higher walls between "us" and "them."

We have more information than ever about the increasing needs, but less time to help. Increasingly, we are daunted by the overwhelming environmental and sociopolitical problems we face. But even with our awareness of our current difficulties, we would be buoyed by each other's stories of faith, determination, and achievement. The truth is that we are in the company of a multitude of spirited women, and once we realize this, there isn't anything we can't do.

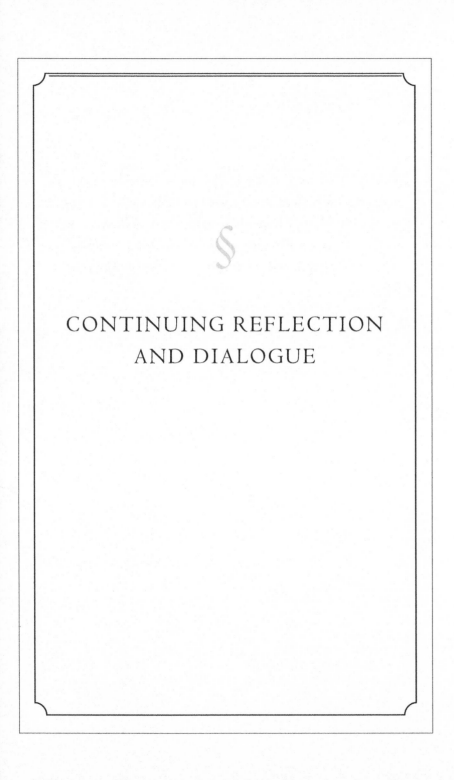

CONTINUING REFLECTION
AND DIALOGUE

About This Guide

These questions and dialogue prompts are provided to encourage your own further reflection and to guide you in sharing your story with others. I hope these suggestions will enrich your reading of *Faith and Feminism* and will help you work toward a sense of wholeness and connection in yourself and all your relationships.

Chapter 1

To Build a Dialogue

§

Continuing Reflection

There are two ways of knowing. Rational knowing, where you understand something with your mind, and experiential knowing, where you have a visceral experience that enables you to feel your understanding on a different level. Reading this book is an invitation to explore both ways of knowing. As ideas about faith and feminism are explored in each chapter, there will be questions in this Reading Group Guide that will give you the opportunity to reflect on the subject and perhaps know it in a different way. I encourage you to obtain a blank journal so that you are able to record your own thoughts and feelings. You can also share your insights with others as a way of making them more real to you. Whether you are in pairs or in a small group, the act of speaking your thoughts out loud and hearing what others are experiencing assists us all not only in becoming united with others, but in grounding more fully into ourselves. The purpose of each of these questions is simply to launch your exploration so that you can discover hidden gems that will help you deliberately create a life that you love. Reflect on these questions:

1. From your own personal experience, do you feel that your spiritual faith and your feminism share common goals or ideals?

2. Do you recall instances in your life when organized religion has not been a supporter of women's rights? How did you feel at those moments? Did it seem as if the concept "men are more valuable" was the unspoken message in your religious upbringing? If so, how has this belief affected your spiritual life?

3. Do you agree or disagree with the sentence: "We must be wary of the perverse application of scripture for the purpose of . . . keep[ing] people divided and excluded"? Can you think of examples from our own time when scripture has been used in this divisive way?

Dialogue

Find a partner or a small group of people who are willing to reflect on the relationship between faith and feminism. Set up time to share your stories with one another. As you discuss these concepts with others, notice how the conversation flows. What is the balance between talking and listening? How does the quality of each feel? A few comments on the steps and meaning of dialogue will follow the questions below, beginning with Chapter 2.

Chapter 2

The Journey Toward Wholeness

§

Continuing Reflection

Think about the women, both those you know and those you know about, who have had a positive impact on your life, the ones you would consider your role models. Choose a page in your journal to write down the names of these women, noting what qualities about them you most admire. Was their personal faith a part of what fortified them and their lives? Then reflect on the following:

1. What are the ways you are like your role models or feel you are becoming like them? What qualities do they have that you would most like to possess in your life?

2. Is spirituality an important part of your life? If so, how would you describe your experience of God? Are there ways you wish it were different?

3. How do you relate to the idea that our "holes," or weaknesses can become areas of strength? Are personal imperfections ever of value to people who

want to make the world a better place? If they are of value, in what ways do you see these life challenges as contributing to the journey toward wholeness?

Dialogue

Find a partner or a small group, and share your reflections with them. Use the process of Dialogue. The three-step Dialogue process goes from mirroring to validation to empathy. The first step, mirroring, is a way of ensuring that you really understand what someone is sharing with you. When you mirror someone, you state back to them what you heard them say, sometimes in their words and sometimes in your own words, though being very careful not to change the meaning of what they shared. While this sounds simple, it is actually difficult to master. Most often, instead of really listening to someone else, we are formulating our own response to what they are saying or are thinking of things in our own lives that the other person's words have evoked in our mind. Mirroring requires a slowing down so we are able to be present with another. Practice exchanging your thoughts with one another, and each of you mirror carefully what the other says. Notice how it quiets you down at your core.

Chapter 3

EMILY DICKINSON
1830–1886

Claiming Your Pain

§

Continuing Reflection

How do you relate to the idea that becoming a more whole person involves experiencing pain? Think about a painful time in your past, adopting the attitude of an explorer who can look upon past scenes of your life without taking them personally. With the benefit of hindsight, allow yourself to focus on this one event in your journal, describing it in detail. Write out all the ways this painful experience affected you. Most likely you'll begin with the hurt or anger associated with that time. Allow yourself to dig deeper. Are there feelings of unfairness or perhaps fear? Are there other treasures that are there, along with these feelings, treasures that maybe you weren't able to see because the feelings eclipsed them? Then ask yourself:

1. Assuming that pain can be a great teacher, can you think of things you've learned from your own painful experiences? Can you think of ways that your pain has opened you to the suffering of others?

2. How do you typically respond to the pain of others? Do you want to fix it, take it away, or let it be? Do you think your responses will be different in the future now that you've had a chance to think about the positive role that pain can play in a person's life?

3. In what ways do you think of Emily as a feminist? Does a particular image come to mind when you think about what a feminist is? Do you consider feminists to be strong or weak? Does your image of them have physical characteristics? Can you describe what it means to you to be a feminist?

4. How can your feminism and your faith coexist? How can they strengthen the other?

Dialogue

If you wish, share your reflections with a partner or a small group. In doing so, use Intentional Dialogue. After you mirror, move into validation, which is an excellent tool when responding to people who are in an extreme emotional state that pain often causes. In the validation process, you are telling a person that it is okay for them to feel the way they do. Period. If pain is ever going to be a teacher for us, we need to first accept that we feel it, and being validated by another helps us do that. It is at this point that the healing process can truly begin.

Chapter 4

TERESA OF ÁVILA

(1515–1582)

Integrating Your Shadow

Continuing Reflection

When moving into the realm of the shadow, imagine yourself as a historian, unearthing dusty treasures that have been forgotten or possibly never before recorded. Take a few moments to think of an aspect of yourself that you've kept hidden. It could be something you identify as positive, such as developing an artistic talent or being a galvanizing force around an important issue. Or it can be something you identify as negative, such as anger or an overly competitive nature. Write down in your journal these previously hidden aspects of yourself. Why do you think you've kept these parts of yourself hidden? If you can, without thinking about your answer, fill in the blanks in this sentence: I chose not to explore _____ (an aspect of myself that is hidden) because _____ (your reason). Then reflect on the following questions:

Continuing Reflection and Dialogue

1. Have you been aware of your own inner struggles where you were pushed or pulled in seemingly opposite directions? How could you have classified each end that you felt pulled between? Was one pole focused more on what Teresa would consider worldly desires and the other on spiritual impulses? Or was one pole about your needs and the other about the needs of someone you love? How did you handle those experiences?

2. Who are the people who have most irritated you? What is it about them that you have found most frustrating? Do you see any patterns between the behaviors that you find irritating and feedback you've received from others about what they find challenging about you?

3. In "Four Waters" Teresa describes the stages of spiritual enlightenment metaphorically through the image of nurturing a garden. How might you describe your spiritual journey metaphorically? Might it be like the stages of mountain climbing, the surrender to the creative process like throwing a clay pot, or the engagement of a physical activity like swimming in the ocean? Can you draw your spiritual journey in pictorial form?

152

Dialogue

Share your reflections with a partner or a small group. When you share, ask someone to use the dialogue process with you. After they mirror and validate, they need to then move into empathy. Empathy is the third and final step in the Intentional Dialogue process. It is a particularly useful tool for shadow work. When empathizing with another person, you are actually feeling how they would feel and letting them know their feelings make sense. Empathy is the visceral experience that deepens from the logical understanding during the mirroring step. Our forgiveness of ourselves grows as we learn to empathize with others. And since what irritates you about someone else is probably an aspect of yourself that you haven't owned yet, it is better for your own sake to approach that person with empathy!

Chapter 5

SOJOURNER TRUTH
(1797–1883)

Finding Your Voice

§

Continuing Reflection

Each one of us has the power of voice, but typically, it is the lecturers, singers, and motivational speakers who consciously reflect and build on this power. Describe in your journal how you feel you use your voice. On a scale of one to ten, with one being the least comfortable and ten being the most comfortable, where would you score when speaking to a large group? Speaking with someone one on one? Do you think your sense of self would be strengthened if you became more intentional about the deepening and amplification of your voice? Also use your journal to explore the following:

1. What do you understand the difference to be between the inner and outer voice? How is each formed? Which do you feel more comfortable with?

2. At this point, you've had the opportunity to meet some of the pain in your life and your shadow side

more completely than before. How do you think this will affect your ability to speak your mind? Do you think you will be able to be more honest?

3. Sojourner Truth also named herself, choosing a name that she felt expressed the essence of who she was. How do you feel about your name? Does it fit? Is it the one that you were given originally or a nickname, or have you changed your name? If you were to create a new name for yourself, what name would you choose, and why? In your journal, describe your name and what it represents. How would you hope to be different after you named yourself? What would you want about yourself to remain the same?

Dialogue

When our voice is heard and accepted, we grow strong. Take some time with your dialogue partner or within your group to freely express what is in your heart, using the three steps of the Dialogue process with each other when it is your turn to listen. How did it feel to be mirrored, validated, and empathized with? Do you feel a difference when someone mirrors you? Do you feel your own voice moving into deeper resonance? Taking the time and care for dialogue is a way we help one another move into strength and authenticity.

Chapter 6

LUCRETIA MOTT
(1793–1880)
Taking Action

§

Continuing Reflection

Action comes in many forms. Like Lucretia, we can become consummate directors of our own lives, scripting our words and creating the sets in ways that enable us to have a profound impact on the lives we touch. Stay-at-home parents are, perhaps, some of the most under-acknowledged directors, as are nurses and teachers. When you look at your life, do you feel that you are doing the things that are important to you? On a page in your journal, write down all the things you would like to be doing. Then write down all the things you are doing. How similar are those lists? As director of your own life, how might you redirect your activities to be more in synch with your talents and passions? What settings would best enhance what you want to offer the world? Would you build organizations or go to work for one that already exists? What roles would you want to cast yourself in—homemaker, activist, author? Who would be your supporting cast and which props would you choose to enrich your life? After you reflect on this, think also about the following:

1. What does the sentence: "Doing is how you come into being" mean to you? Can you think of an incident in your own life that supports the statement? What was the action you took? And how did that action ultimately help move you into greater wholeness?

2. What do you think Lucretia meant when she talked about being a messiah of your own age? How is it that you feel called to impact the world?

3. What does the phrase "all that an impartial Creator has bestowed" mean to you? How do you feel God wants your life to both represent and further greater equality and justice?

Dialogue

When discussing the questions above with your dialogue partner or group, continue using the experience as a chance to practice intentional dialogue. True dialogue, mirroring, validation, and empathy seem to go hand in hand with action. Being mirrored helps to coalesce the energy of the psyche, strengthen the self, and support action. Identify the life goals that you want to achieve, and share them while another listens with the tools of intentional dialogue.

Chapter 7

DOROTHY DAY

(1897–1980)

Living Communion

§

Continuing Reflection

In the midst of crowded cities and an overpopulated world, the feeling of isolation and alienation is common to us all. But then there are those with whom we experience a deep communion. Who are these people in your life and what qualities do they have that allow you to feel close to them? Write about them in your journal, identifying the specific ways that those relationships have enriched your life. In addition think about the following:

1. Were you to start a Hospitality House, who would you want to serve and where would it be located? How would your Hospitality House minister to others and what would your role in it be? Are there ways you are creating communion already in your own life?

2. Dorothy's assertion that you should not write (or speak) about things unless you are willing to assume

the obligations that go with them is very tough. What do you think she meant, and do you agree with her?

3. What do you feel is the connection between the acts of accepting your pain and integrating your shadow, finding your voice and taking action, and the capacity for understanding and compassion?

Dialogue

Spend some time reflecting on the questions above with your dialogue partner or in your group. Has Dorothy's story affected your experience of empathy? Share any insights out loud. As you do so, be aware that as you dialogue with one or more persons, you are creating sacred space among you. Spend time being present with one another. Feel the world slowing down and your heart opening up.

Chapter 8

Weaving a Connection

§

Continuing Reflection

Faith and Feminism is about the power of individual stories and an invitation to you to reflect on yours. Formulating our auto-biographies makes us clarify what we believe and what we think about abstract concepts, such as religion, feminism, and social action. Articulating our story is a useful exercise, whether we ever publish the story or not. Our awareness of ourselves grows as we tell our stories. We see patterns emerge that might have remained hidden to us. Telling our stories helps us live more deliberate lives, lives based on choices we make consciously. Now that I have shared mine with you, you are invited to explore your own story. In your journal, draft a five- to seven-page biography. How would you define yourself? What life experiences have shaped who you are? What is important for others to know about you? What have you struggled with? What do you feel your story can teach others? Then reflect on the following:

1. When you write or share your story, listen to what you choose to emphasize or ignore, and how you

choose to express yourself. How you share your story shapes it. What did the act of telling the story teach you about yourself?

2. Many women have gained further insight into themselves by drawing a chart, diagram, or design that represents their life journey. If you were to draw one, what would it look like? On your diagram, you could indicate the important events in your life, your important relationships, the dark times, and the happy times.

3. Would you say you have a calling in life? Has it changed over time, or has it remained the same? Where has this sense of calling come from? How were you created and what is your relationship with that creative force? What would you like it to be?

4. What action can you take in your life to weave your faith into contributions to improve our society?

5. How might you lean on the support of your faith community to contribute to the feminist agenda? What have you learned in your faith community that would serve the cause of social activism?

Dialogue

The stories of many women in history have been forgotten. Be aware of how important it is that your story does not get lost—lost to yourself as well as those around you. Practice telling your story in your group or with your dialogue partner. Note how it feels to have them mirror, validate, and empathize with those aspects of your story you find challenging and those you feel more proud of. Also, take some time to explore with your dialogue partner what you feel the next stage of your journey is. Do you feel moved to express both the faith and feminism parts of your nature? What new actions might this entail? What are the specific steps you could take?

APPENDIX A: RESOURCE GUIDE

Amherst Academy
(Now Amherst College)
Amherst College
Amherst, MA 01002-5000
www.amherst.edu

The Call
1539 East Howard Street
Pasadena, CA 91104
Phone: 626-296-7940
www.thecallrevolution.com

Carmelite Order
Carmelite Institute
1600 Webster Street, NE
Washington, D.C. 20017
Phone: 202-635-3534
www.carmelites.info

The Catholic Worker
36 East First Street
New York, NY 10003
Phone: 212-777-9617
www.catholicworker.org

House of Hospitality
(The Catholic Worker listings)
The Catholic Worker
36 East First Street
New York, NY 10003
Phone: 212-777-9617

www.catholicworker.org/communities/commlistall.cfm

Human Rights Watch,
Women's Rights Division
350 Fifth Avenue, 34th Floor
New York, NY 10118-3299
Phone: 212-290-4700

www.hrw.org

Imago
Imago Relationships International
335 North Knowles Avenue
Winter Park, FL 32789
Phone: 407-644-4937

www.imagotherapy.com

Indigenous Women's Network
Annette Looks Twice
Program Director
13621 FM 2769
Austin, TX 78726
Phone: 512-258-3880
www.honorearth.org

Ms. Foundation for Women
120 Wall Street, 33rd Floor
New York, NY 10005
Phone: 212-742-2300
www.ms.foundation.org

Appendix A: Resource Guide

New York Women's Foundation
NYWF
34 West 22nd Street
New York, NY 10010
Phone: 212-414-4342
www.nywf.org

National Organization for Women
(NOW)
733 15th Street, NW, 2nd Floor
Washington, D.C. 20005
www.now.org

Pax Christi International
Rue du Vieux Marché aux Grains, 21
1000 Brussels
Belgium
Phone: 32-02-502-55-50
www.paxchristi.net

San Francisco Women's Foundation (recently merged into
The Women's Foundation of California)
The Women's Foundation of California
340 Pine Street, Suite 302
San Francisco, CA 94104
Phone: 415-837-1113
www.womensfoundca.org

The Sister Fund
116 East 16th Street, 7th Floor
New York, NY 10003
Phone: 212-260-4446
www.sisterfund.org

Socialist Party

339 Lafayette Street, No. 303

New York, NY 10012

Phone: 212-982-4586

www.sp-usa.org

Society of Friends

1216 Arch St., No. 2B

Philadelphia, PA 19107

www.fgcquaker.org

Stone Center

Stone Center for Developmental Services and Studies

Wellesley College

106 Central Street

Wellesley, MA 02481

Phone: 781-283-2500

www.wcwonline.org/w-stone.html

Take Our Daughters to Work Day

Take Our Daughters and Sons to Work

Ms. Foundation for Women

120 Wall Street, 33rd Floor

New York, NY 10005

Phone: 212-742-2300, ext. 4429

www.daughtersandsonstowork.org

Teresian Sisters

OCD General House

Corso d'Italia,

38 - 00198 Roma

Italia

www.ocd.pcn.net *Also:* www.carmelnuns.com

Union Theological Seminary

3041 Broadway at 121st Street
New York, NY 10027

Phone: 212-662-7100

www.uts.columbia.edu

United Farm Workers

National Headquarters
P.O. Box 62
Keene, CA 93531

www.ufw.org

U.N. World Conference on Women

United Nations
New York, NY 10017

Phone: 212-963-4664

www.un.org/womenwatch

Vatican II

www.vatican.va/archive/index.htm

Women and Public Policy Program

John F. Kennedy School of Government
79 JFK Street
Cambridge, MA 02138

Phone: 617-496-6973

www.ksg.harvard.edu/wappp

Women for Afghan Women

35-32 Union Street, 2nd Floor
Flushing, NY 11354

Phone: 718-321-2434

www.womenforafghanwomen.org

Women's Funding Network

1375 Sutter Street, Suite 406
San Francisco, CA 94109

Phone: 415-441-0706

www.wfnet.org

Women's Hall of Fame

National Women's Hall of Fame
76 Fall Street
P.O. Box 335
Seneca Falls, NY 13148

Phone: 315-568-8060

www.greatwomen.org

APPENDIX B: TIMELINE

New Testament: Early Christian women, such as Phoebe and Priscilla, act as deacons and take on leadership roles in spreading Jesus' words.

1200s–1400s: Women called the Beguines begin a Christian lay women's movement in the Low Countries. Some scholars call it the first women's movement in the West.

1515–1582: Teresa of Ávila

1793–1880: Lucretia Mott

1797–1883: Sojourner Truth

1830–1886: Emily Dickinson

1837: First Anti-Slavery Convention of American Women is held. Women work to enter public life to abolish slavery. Issued first public call for women's rights.

1838: Second Anti-Slavery Convention of American Women. As backlash, the next year, the convention hall was burned to the ground.

1848: Women's Rights Convention at Seneca Falls. Declaration of Sentiments includes first call for women's suffrage.

1865: Civil War ends and the Emancipation Proclamation frees American slaves from slavery.

1876: British Common Law (which also extended to Canada and Australia at the time) stated that women were people in matters of "pains and penalties" but not in "rights and privileges."

1897–1980: Dorothy Day

1920: Women in the U.S. secure the right to vote.

1923: The first Equal Rights Amendment (ERA), called the Lucretia Mott Amendment at the time in honor of Mott, is introduced in Congress. It has been introduced in Congress every session since.

1929: The British law stating that women were not legally people was finally overturned (on appeal), after it was challenged by Emily Murphy, the first female magistrate in the British Empire. She was inspired to do this after a defendant's attorney claimed she was not a person and therefore not able to perform the duties of a magistrate.

1960s: Robin Morgan coins the phrase "The personal is political."

1966: National Organization of Women (NOW) founded.

1972: Ms. Foundation for Women founded. ERA passes Congress. It was ratified by thirty-five states, but it was not ratified by the necessary thirty-eight states by the July 1982 deadline.

1980s: Feminist theology begins as a field. Carol Gilligan coins the phrase "not knowing what you know," which refers to people splitting their thoughts from their feelings.

1985: Women's Funding Network, formerly called National Network of Women's Funds, was founded.

1987: New York Women's Foundation was founded.

1993: The Sister Fund founded.

1995: United Nations Fourth World Conference on Women in Beijing, China.

NOTES

Letter to the Reader

1. The Beguines flourished in the Low Countries in the thirteenth century. They came together on their own to live out their understanding that Christianity was more than a collection of dogmas; it was a way of life in which the Gospel's demands were relevant not just to the ordained, but to everyone, including women. At a time when the theological education of women was nonexistent and condemned as scandalous because of the "weakness of their intellect," the Beguines were actively writing and teaching in the communities they served. Marguerite Porete was burned at the stake in 1310 for disseminating her work *The Mirror of Simple Souls*. Her writing, and that of others, developed a special kind of mysticism, *mine-mysteik* (love mysticism), which was a homespun theology centered on the nonrational and numinous aspects of God. While the Beguines flourished in the thirteenth century, in the fourteenth century, they were condemned as heretical.

2. Bernard McGinn is one of several medieval scholars who reference the Beguines as the earliest large-scale emergence of women's voices in the history of Christian thought.

In Bernard McGinn, *Meister Eckart and the Beguine Mystics: Hadewijch of Brabant, Mechthild of Magdeburg, and Marguerite Porete* (New
York: Continuum, 1994).

3. A fine overview of this field is found in Andrew Kadel,
*Matrology: A Bibliography of Writings by Christian Women from the
First to the Fifteenth Centuries* (New York: Continuum, 1995).

4. As to the time at Hildegard's monastery, I recall one
interesting story. Hans, the guide I found, had lived his whole
life around Bingen and knew the countryside like the back of
his hand and was eager to share the beauty and history of his
country with me. I was amazed, upon asking about Hildegard,
to find that he'd never even heard of her! He made the shift
from guide to co-explorer, and the two of us researched the
places where Hildegard had lived and worked. Hans took
notes as we stopped at various places, looking forward to taking others to these sites. He was affected by the story of
Hildegard, a thirteenth-century nun, who had been lost to history for five hundred years. Hildegard was rediscovered in the
1930s.

Another unrecognized woman is Kateri Tekakwitha
(1656–1680), a Mohawk Indian whose father was a Mohawk
chief. Her father insisted she marry a powerful man within the
tribe, but she chose instead an inner life of prayer and contemplation and was eventually recognized as a saint. One day, I
was walking down Fifth Avenue in New York when I glanced
over at St. Patrick's Cathedral. I noticed that one of the saints
depicted in bas-relief on the front door was Kateri. I walked
inside and asked what they could tell me about the saint on
that door. No one inside could tell me anything about Kateri.

These two stories illustrate a danger that the stories of exceptional women will be lost and forgotten. Phoebe Palmer, a nineteenth-century Holiness Revivalist, offered, "The church in many places is a sort of potters' field where the gifts of many women, as so many strangers, are buried."

5. For an excellent summary of Black Madonna sites and their meaning in relation to progressive political activism, see Lucia Birnbaum's study, *Black Madonnas: Feminism, Religion, and Politics in Italy* (Boston: Northeastern University Press, 1993). Also, China Galland's books *Longing for Darkness* and *The Bond Between Women* offer discussion of the connection between Black Madonna sites and nonviolent activism throughout Eastern Europe.

6. In addition, I visited St. Clare's Cathedral in Assisi, the cathedral where Catherine of Siena is buried, and stood on the steps of the Lincoln Memorial, imagining the meeting between Sojourner Truth and President Lincoln.

7. I studied with women-centered theologians Drs. Janet Walton and Delores Williams of Union Theological Seminary.

8. CHUNG, Hyun Kyung (*Struggle to Be the Sun Again*), Ada María Isasi-Díaz (*En la Lucha*), emilie townes (*A Troubling in My Soul*), and Paula Gunn Allen (*The Sacred Hoop*), look to weave women's experience more directly into their faith practice.

9. I Corinthians: 13.

10. Harville is a gifted theorist who has constructed a theory of relationship consciousness called Imago. Early in our relationship Harville discussed how marriage held the best potential for helping a couple heal their individual childhood

wounds. Material written by Harville alone or by us together has been translated into forty different languages, and 1,700 therapists have been trained to offer Imago therapy in thirteen foreign countries.

Chapter 1. To Build a Dialogue

1. The conference in Beijing was the first U.N. World Conference on Women to include spirituality and religion as topics of discussion.

2. I created and administered this study as a course with Dr. Delores Williams at Union Theological Seminary.

3. Wilma Montanez commented on the value of recognizing that "if you leave faith out of the organizing, you leave Hispanic women out."

4. A statement made by Robin Morgan, a leading second wave author and activist.

5. One example is Anne Llewellyn Barstow's work, where she draws parallels between the current circumstances that women face today and witch hunts, citing materials from India as being the most similar. Anne Llewellyn Barstow, *Witchcraze: A New History of the European Witch Hunts* (San Francisco: Pandora, 1994).

6. The National Organization for Women (NOW) exposed the antiwomen tactics of organized religion. But it also structured and founded a national committee for feminists and faith-based institutions. While it is not commonly known, there were many women of faith who created the resurgence of feminism in the 1970s. NOW had its founding meeting on the campus of a Catholic women's college, Alverno, in Mil-

waukee, and one of the founders, Sister Joel Reed, was from Alverno. The coalitions for the equal rights amendment were greatly enhanced by the support of many churches and religious groups. Secular and faith-based women worked side by side on the ERA in spite of the fact that the amendment raised some "dangerous" issues, such as abortion, birth control, and same-sex marriages. See Ann Braude's work at Harvard Divinity School for more information.

7. The catchphrase "women are people too" came from periods throughout history in which women had to fight second-class citizenship. One recent example concerned both Canadian and Australian women, who were defined by the 1876 British Common Law ruling: "Women are persons in matter of pains and penalties, but are not persons in matters of rights and privileges." Women were not permitted to participate fully in public offices or affairs of state. In 1916, Judge Emily Murphy, the first female magistrate in the British Empire, found herself challenged in court by a defendant's lawyer who claimed that she was not a person and therefore not able to perform the duties of magistrate. In the spring of 1928, Emily Murphy and four other women appealed to the Supreme Court of Canada to consider this question: "Does the word 'person' . . . include female 'persons'?" The Supreme Court answered, "No, it does not." They appealed this ruling, and finally, on October 18, 1929, the Lord Chancellor of the Privy Council announced the unanimous decision of the five lords on the council that "the exclusion of women from all public offices is a relic of days more barbarous than ours."

8. *Turning the World Upside Down,* 11.

9. Angelina Grimke to William Lloyd Garrison, 30 Aug. 1837, in *Liberator,* 19 Sept. 1835.

10. *Turning the World Upside Down,* 13.

11. Virginia Bernhard and Elizabeth Fox-Genovese, *The Birth of American Feminism: The Seneca Falls Convention of 1848* (St James, N.Y.: Brandywine Press, 1995), 79.

12. Elizabeth Cady Stanton, *Eighty Years or More: Reminiscences, 1815–1897* (Boston: Northeastern University Press, 1993 [1898]).

13. Judith Jordan et al. *Women's Growth in Connection: Writings from the Stone Center* (New York: Guilford Press, 1991). See especially Jean Baker Miller, pp. 13–20, and Janet Surrey, pp. 52–56. Judith Jordan, Jean Baker Miller, Irene Stiver, Janet L. Surrey, and Alexandra G. Kaplan have written extensively about the different patterns of development followed by male and female children. They maintain that female infants and children evolve an identity while remaining in relationship with their context (beginning with their mothers). Males, on the other hand, are encouraged to separate from their context. They are given the message that they must individuate in order to become themselves. Women are given the opposite message.

Chapter 2. The Journey Toward Wholeness

1. Isaiah 43:1.

2. Galatians 3:15.

3. This phrase comes from the Indigenous Women's Network.

4. Mary Rose O'Reilley, *Radical Presence: Teaching as Contemplative Practice* (Portsmouth, N.H.: Boynton/Cook Publishers, 1998), 23.

5. Jean Houston, Jean Shinoda-Bolin, China Galland, and others have attempted to delineate more clearly the women's journey. Also when I refer to the "feminine" and the "masculine," I don't mean the characteristics that are innate and set by biology. I refer to the constructivist view, which recognizes the centrality of the social construction of gender. See Nancy R. Goldberger, et al., eds., *Knowledge, Difference, and Power* (New York: Basic Books, 1996). Many people have found Campbell's description of the hero's journey to be too focused on the individual's solitary achievement to be an adequate description of heroism in women. Women are socialized to be aware of the role that social context has played in the course of their lives. See Judith Jordan et al., *Women's Growth in Connection* (New York: Guilford Press, 1991).

6. Theorist Carol Gilligan has analyzed how common it is for people to separate their thoughts from their feelings. They end up "not knowing what they know." They disassociate their inner world from their outer world. I have been interested in understanding how we can achieve more inner-outer congruence and how our daily actions can better match the ethics we espouse.

Chapter 3. Emily Dickinson: Claiming Your Pain

1. Richard B. Sewall, *The Life of Emily Dickinson* (New York: Farrar, Straus & Giroux, 1980), 378.

2. Ibid., 57.

3. Robin Morgan, *The Word of a Woman: Feminist Dispatches 1968–1982* (New York: W. W. Norton & Co., 1992), 158.

4. Sewall, 360–61.

5. Ibid., 564.

6. Ibid., 556.

7. Ibid., 491.

8. Jean Houston, *Public Like a Frog: Entering the Lives of Three Great Americans* (Wheaton, Ill.: Quest Books, 1993), 39.

9. The democratization of religion is well described in Nathan Hatch's book *The Democratization of American Christianity* (New Haven: Yale University Press, 1989). He points out that in the seventeenth and eighteenth centuries, religion in America underwent a democratization—along with society—the effect of which was the relocation of authority (p. 3). For the believer, this meant that God's will was manifest in the individual. In this context of religious disestablishment, women reformers rose up and spoke out from a personal religious vision.

10. Sewall, 643.

11. Ibid., 23.

12. Ibid., 424.

13. Ibid., 390.

14. Ibid., 461.

15. Ibid., 636.

16. Ibid., 462.

17. Ibid., 589.

18. Wilhelm/Baynes, *The I Ching or Book of Changes*, the Richard Wilhelm Translation rendered into English by Cary F.

Baynes, Bollingen Series XIX (Princeton, N.J.: Princeton University Press, 1967), 237 (paraphrase).

19. Houston, 69.

20. Kathleen Norris, *The Cloister Walk* (New York: Riverhead Books, 1996), 94.

21. Sewall, 674.

Chapter 4. Teresa of Ávila: Integrating Your Shadow

1. "Shadow" is a term made popular by Carl Jung. It describes those aspects of ourselves that we have denied or disowned. While unseen by us, they can be obvious to those around us. It is often our closest friends, partners, and children who offer us insight into our shadows. While it may be difficult to see our shadow, it offers us keys to our wholeness. Our inner power is often hidden away in the depths of our shadow, along with other talents and qualities.

2. Allison E. Peers, ed., introduction to *The Life of Teresa of Jesus: The Autobiography of Teresa of Ávila* (Garden City, N.Y.: Image Books, 1950), 40.

3. Tessa Bielecki, *Holy Daring: An Outrageous Gift to Modern Spirituality from Saint Teresa the Grand Wild Woman of Ávila* (Rockport, Mass.: Element Publishing, 1994), 12.

4. John Baptist Rossi (Prior General of the Carmelite Order from 1562 until his death in 1578).

5. Mary Hester Valentine, *Saints for Contemporary Women* (Chicago: Thomas More Press, 1987), 85.

6. Victoria Lincoln, *Teresa, a Woman: A Biography of Teresa of Ávila* (Albany, N.Y.: Albany State University Press, 1984), 15.

7. Ibid.

8. Lincoln, 8.

9. St. Teresa of Ávila, *The Life*, 108–109.

10. Ibid., 109.

11. Ibid., 81.

12. Ibid., 112.

13. Lincoln, 29.

14. St. Teresa of Ávila, *The Life*, 110.

15. Anne Gordon, *Book of Saints* (New York: Bantam Books, 1994), 148.

16. Lincoln, 20.

17. The Discalced Carmelite Order of Friars currently has 20 communities nationwide, with 171 priests and brothers. The Discalced Carmelite Order of Nuns has 65 active communities in the U.S. with 875 sisters. Discalced Seculars (the Third Order) has 75 groups in the U.S., with 3,000 members (Sister Constance Fitzgerald, personal interview, 29 Nov. 1996); see Sister Catherine Marie Bazar and Sister Michael Marie Zobelien, *Teresa of Ávila* (Seattle: Carmelite Nuns, 1981).

18. The Society of St. Teresa of Jesus currently has 8 communities in the U.S. with 50 sisters, and 209 communities worldwide, with approximately 2,000 sisters (Sister Carla at the Society of St. Teresa of Jesus, Convington, La., interview, 22 Nov. 1996). See www.victorshepherd.on.ca/Heritage/teresaof.htm.

19. Dorothy wrote: "I had read the life of St. Teresa of Ávila and had fallen in love with her. . . . she wore a bright red dress when she entered the convent, which made me love her and feel close to her." *The Long Loneliness* (San Francisco: HarperCollins, 1997), 140.

20. A good reference on Debbie Ford's work is *The Secret of the Shadow* (San Francisco: HarperCollins, 2002). Ford integrates much we have learned about shadow work.

Chapter 5. Sojourner Truth: Finding Your Voice

1. The inspiration for this chapter on voice is Carol Gilligan's groundbreaking work *In a Different Voice: Psychological Theory and Women's Development* (Cambridge, Mass.: Harvard University Press, 1982). Gilligan is known for her studies on the difficulty adolescent girls have in finding their sense of voice and its impact on their psychological development. For her, voicing is selfing, and the cultivating and strengthening of voice is essential to women's psychological maturity.

2. Sojourner, as well as other young women who struggle to overcome silence, may be criticized for their lack of voice, but Gilligan and others see young women's silence as "healthy resistance" to an oppressive patriarchal society. In "Embodying Knowledge, Knowing Desire: Authority and Split Subjectivities in Girls' Epistemological Development," Elizabeth DeBold, Deborah Tolman, and Lyn Mikel Brown further expound on the work of Carol Gilligan by arguing that "the transformations in girls' selves and relationships in early adolescence, and arguably again at the end of their high school experience, place these girls under pressure to conform—to subject themselves—to cultural standards that do not embrace either the reality or complexity of their experience." Girls then may act out or withdraw. Rather than assuming that they are a problem and are in need of correction, it is important to see their actions and/or withdrawal as their refusal to submit to the patriarchy. Nancy Goldberger et al., *Knowledge, Difference, and Power: Essays Inspired by Women's Way of Knowing* (New York: Basic Books, 1996), 96.

3. Jacqueline Bernard, *Journey Toward Freedom: The Story of Sojourner Truth* (New York: Feminist Press, 1990), 2.

4. Ibid., 4–8.

5. Susan Taylor-Boyd, *Sojourner Truth: The Courageous Former Slave Whose Eloquence Helped Promote Human Equality* (Harrisburg, Pa.: Morehouse Publishing Co., 1990), 6.

6. Bernard, 7.

7. Ibid., 36–37.

8. Ibid., 116.

9. Ibid., 122.

10. Beginning in the nineteenth century, women like Sojourner felt "called" to revolution. A call is a bridge between the ordinary and the extraordinary. Something occurs, an event or a sign, and the ordinary person is summoned to a great adventure. Women were active in issues of temperance, abolition of slavery, equal education, and the right to vote. Through decades of the next century, the "call" deepened and broadened to include the wide array of psychological, sociological, economic, and spiritual issues that affected the quality of life for all women.

11. The convention cited was the Ohio Women's Rights Convention, convened in the Stone Church in Akron at 10 A.M. on May 28, 1851. The excerpt here was taken from a report by Marius Robinson. He was a friend of Sojourner's and was also acting as the secretary of the convention. Nell Irvin Painter, *Sojourner Truth: A Life* (New York: Norton, 1997), 125.

12. Bernard, 152.

13. In Nell Irvin Painter, "Sojourner Truth," in *Facts on File Encyclopedia of Black Women in America: The Early Years, 1619–1899* (New York: Facts on File, 1997), 174–75.

14. Bernard, 175.

15. Taylor-Boyd, 43.

16. Painter, 84.

17. Isaiah 58:1.

18. Bernard, 202.

19. Schweickart offers an analogy, that "the importance of the receptive role becomes evident when we shift to written communication where the moment of assertion, writing, is detached from the moment of reception, reading, and both are reduced to silence, so that neither appears to be more nor less active than the other. . . . At the moment of reading, the reader, the only human agent present, is the producer of meaning. While it is easy to think of listening as doing nothing, everyone will agree that reading often takes considerable time and effort, and that comprehension does not happen mechanically."

Silence grows more golden when Schweickart reveals the subtle importance of listening, clarifying that "the silence of the listener does not mean that she is doing nothing and producing nothing (to the extent that she is doing nothing, she is *not* listening). Like the reader, she is actively engaged in producing the meaning of the other's utterances." Schweickart likens the speaker to the writer and the listener to the reader. By looking at the active role of the reader, she implies that the listener is equally active and that the listener, like the reader, is a meaning maker.

Patrocinio Schweickart, "Speech Is Silver, Silence Is Gold: The Asymmetrical Intersubjectivity of Communicative Action," in *Knowledge, Difference, and Power: Essays Inspired by Women's Ways of Knowing,* Nancy Rule Goldberger, et al., eds. (New York: Basic Books, 1996), 318–19.

20. Nelle K. Morton, "The Rising of Women's Consciousness in Male Language Structure," *Andover Newton Quarterly* 12, Number 4 (March 1972), 177–90.

Chapter 6. Lucretia Mott: Taking Action

1. In 1923, in Seneca Falls for the celebration of the seventy-fifth anniversary of the 1848 Women's Rights Convention, Alice Paul introduced the Lucretia Mott Amendment, with the aim of affirming the equal application of the Constitution to all citizens. It was introduced into every session of Congress until it passed in 1972. The amendment read: "Men and women shall have equal rights throughout the United States and every place subject to its jurisdiction."

2. Margaret Hope Bacon, *Valiant Friend* (New York: Walker & Co., 1980), 26.

3. Bacon, 26.

4. Douglas Steere, ed., *Quaker Spirituality: Selected Writings* (Mahwah, N.J.: Paulist Press, 1984), 250. Friends have always believed that men and women have an equal ability to be infused with the spirit of God and an equal ability to communicate their inward holiness.

5. This phrase, used first in 1647 by George Fox, the founder of Quakerism, is one of the fundamental tenets of the Society of Friends.

6. Bacon, 29–33.

7. Ibid., 33.

8. Lucretia was an organizer and an officer of the First Anti-Slavery Convention of American Women held in 1837 in New York City. This was the first national political convention of women and one of the first multiracial meetings held in America. It was at this convention that Lucretia considers the first call to women's rights was made.

9. Elizabeth Cady Stanton, "Lucretia Mott: Eulogy at the Memorial Services Held in Washington by the National Woman Suffrage Association, January 19, 1881," in *The History of Woman Suffrage*, vol. 1, *1848–1861*, ed. Elizabeth Cady Stanton, Susan B. Anthony, and Matilda Joslyn Gage (Rochester, N.Y.: Charles Mann, 1889 [1881]), 420. (This source will henceforth be referred to as Stanton, "Lucretia Mott," *HWS*.)

10. Stanton, "Lucretia Mott," *HWS*, 419.

11. Ibid., 420.

12. Ibid., 420–21.

13. Ibid., 421.

14. Ibid., 422.

15. Ibid., 424.

16. Mott to Stanton, 16 March 1855, in *Selected Letters of Lucretia Coffin Mott*, Beverly Wilson Palmer, ed. (Urbana: University of Illinois Press, 2002), 233.

17. Elizabeth Cady Stanton, *Eighty Years and More: Reminiscences, 1815–1897* (Boston: Northeastern University Press, 1993 [1898]), 194.

18. Bacon, 171.

Chapter 7. Dorothy Day: Living Communion

1. Dorothy's first jail experience occurred around 1918, when she accompanied a group of women suffragists to the White House to advocate a woman's right to vote. Another key reason for her going was that "the women's party who had been picketing and serving jail sentences had been given very brutal treatment, and a committee to uphold the rights of political prisoners had been formed." She describes the jail conditions: "The facilities there were inadequate for so many prisoners. We had to sleep fifteen in a room meant for two, with cots cheek by jowl so that it was impossible to stir." After being sentenced and transported to the prison, Dorothy writes: "Our spokeswoman got up and began to announce that we were all going on hunger strike unless our demands were met, but before she could get the first words out of her mouth . . . the room was filled with men. There were two guards to every woman, and each of us was seized roughly by the arms and dragged out of the room." She describes trying to get to her friend: "I started to cross the room to join her, and was immediately seized by two guards. My instinctive impulse was to pull myself loose, to resist such handling, which only caused the men to tighten their hold on me, even to twist my arms painfully." She continues, "We were then hurled onto some benches and when I tried to pick myself up and again join Peggy in my blind desire to be near a friend, I was thrown to the floor. When another prisoner tried to come to my rescue, we found ourselves in the midst of a milling crowd of guards being pummeled and pushed and kicked and dragged

so that we were scarcely conscious, in shock of what was taking place." Dorothy Day served a thirty-day sentence, which had a crucial impact on her ability to have empathy for the suffering and torture of others. In Dorothy Day, *The Long Loneliness: The Autobiography of Dorothy Day* (San Francisco: HarperCollins, 1997), 72–78.

2. Ibid., 78.

3. Ibid., 89.

4. Ibid., 133.

5. Ibid., 157–58.

6. Robert Coles, *Dorothy Day: A Radical Devotion* (Reading, Mass.: Perseus Books, 1987), 29.

7. In *The Long Loneliness*, p. 185, Dorothy Day writes, "Peter, the 'green' revolutionist, had a long-term program which called for hospices, or houses of hospitality, where the works of mercy could be practiced to combat the taking over by the state of all those services which could be built up by mutual aid; and farming communes to provide land and homes for the unemployed, whom increasing technology was piling up into the millions."

She transformed her apartment in New York into the first hospitality house. In his article "Dorothy Day, the Catholic Worker, and American Pacifism," Charles Chatfield writes that "about 800 'discarded people' a day were fed at the New York house alone in 1937." This article was taken off the Fellowship of Reconciliation Web site, www.forusa.org. Charles Chatfield is a professor of history at Wittenberg University and the author or editor of many books on peace history. A different version of this essay originally appeared in *American Catholic*

Pacifism, edited by Anne Klejment and Nancy Roberts, and appears here with the permission of Praeger Publishers.

8. Day concludes that being at war with oneself is too high a price to pay for anything, which agrees with Socrates, who said that he would "rather be at odds with the whole world than be out of harmony with himself." A good reference on Socrates is Gerald A. Press, ed., *Plato's Dialogues* (Lanham, Md.: Rowman & Littlefield, 1993).

9. Coles, 116.

10. Ibid., 58.

11. This statement is commonly attributed to Day and thought to have been said to an interviewer in the late 1970s.

12. Mary Valentine, *Saints for Contemporary Women* (Chicago: Thomas More Press, 1987), 191.

13. Kim Benito Furumoto, "Diatribe People of Color," *News Collective*, vol. II, no. 4 (May 1993).

14. James Allaire and Rosemary Broughton, *Praying with Dorothy Day Companions for the Journey* (Winona, Minn.: Saint Mary's Press, 1995). (Call 800-533-8095 to order.)

15. Quoted in Jim Forest and Nancy Forest-Flier, "The Trouble with Saint Dorothy," *U.S. Catholic*, 62, no. 11 (Nov. 1997): 18.

16. Commonly attributed to Feodor Dostoyevsky.

Chapter 8. Weaving a Connection

1. For a thoughtful book on the collective voice, where individuals are gathered into choruses that sing for compassion and justice, see Susan Thistlethwaite and Mary Potter Engel, eds., *Lift Every Voice* (Maryknoll, N.Y.: Orbis, 1998).

2. This sense of unity is found in women's funds, where we are in the company of diverse groups of women who are able to speak with a collective voice.

3. Gloria Steinem, "Revaluing Economics," in *Moving Beyond Words: Age, Rage, Sex, Power, Money, Muscles: Breaking Boundaries of Gender* (New York: Simon & Schuster, 1994).

4. Funds "by and for women" that raise money for low-income women and girls are new to history.

5. Along with Tracy, Roma Guy and Marya Grambs were major activists. Other women who made important contributions are Katherine Acey, Stephanie Clohesy, Letty Cottin Pogrebin, Patricia Carbine, and Karen Zellermyer.

6. The Ms. Foundation for Women has been in existence since 1972. It now funds both locally and internationally, and is one of the premier foundations supporting women's rights. One of their more notable accomplishments is the popular Take Our Daughters to Work Day, a campaign created by Nell Merlino.

7. The New York Women's Foundation (NYWF), founded in 1987, works alongside other prominent foundations like the Ms. Foundation for Women. Unlike Ms., which offers national as well as local grants, NYWF focuses on local grant-making within the disenfranchised communities of New York City's five boroughs.

8. Reading the work of Martin Buber, what struck me most deeply was his idea that the average relationship was an I/It where we think of the person we are in relation with as an "It" to meet our needs. He describes another kind of relationship, an I/Thou relationship, where the interest of the other is

foremost. It is the I/Thou relationship that Buber suggests is the carrier of the spirit of God in the world. His writings articulated a yearning that I had felt strongly but had failed to express. This yearning had been with me for as long as I could remember. Until Buber, I had felt it was reflected best by a Dostoyevsky quote that I read in high school. Although I wasn't one to remember quotes, I have remembered these words throughout my life: "The person who seeks the living God face-to-face does not seek God in the empty firmament of his or her mind, but in human love [paraphrase]."

Afterword: Toward a Whole Feminism

1. As stated in the Declaration of Sentiments produced at the Seneca Falls Convention in 1848.

2. See Charlene Spretnak's *Missing Mary: The Queen of Heaven and Her Re-emergence in the Modern Church* (New York: Palgrave Macmillan, 2004) and Elizabeth Johnson's *Truly Our Sister: A Theology of Mary in the Communion of Saints* (New York: Continuum, 2003).

3. Carol Gilligan's work promotes the ethic of caring, balancing it with the ethic of justice, which is held primarily by many men in our culture (*In a Different Voice*, 62).

4. The Agros Foundation is a public charity under section 501(c)(3) of the Internal Revenue Code. Agros Foundation, 4528 8th Avenue, NE, Seattle, WA 98105. You can find out more about their work in South America at their Web site: www.agros.org

5. Sally Roesch Wagner has written on the Iroquois influence on the feminist movement. See her book, *The Untold Story*

of the Iroquois Influence on Early Feminists (Aberdeen, S.Dak.: Sky Carrier Press, 1996).

6. RisingLeaf Watershed Arts is a nonprofit organization based in Carmel, California. For more information about RisingLeaf Watershed Arts and their work, visit their Web site: www.risingleaf.org.

RECOMMENDED READING

Emily Dickinson

Dickinson, Emily. *The Complete Poems of Emily Dickinson*. Edited by Thomas H. Johnson. New York: Little, Brown, 1960.

―――. *Emily Dickinson: Selected Letters*. Edited by Thomas Johnson. Cambridge, Mass.: Belknap Press, 1985.

Houston, Jean. *Public Like a Frog: Entering the Lives of Three Great Americans*. Wheaton, Ill.: Quest Books, 1993.

Sewall, Richard B. *The Life of Emily Dickinson*. New York: Farrar, Straus & Giroux, 1980.

Wolff, Cynthia Griffin. *Emily Dickinson*. New York: Perseus Publishing, 1988.

Teresa of Ávila

Bazar, Sister Catherine Marie, and Sister Michael Marie Zobelien. *Teresa of Ávila: A Valiant Woman*. Seattle: Carmelite Nuns, 1981.

Bielecki, Tessa. *Holy Daring: An Outrageous Gift to Modern Spirituality from Saint Teresa the Grand Wild Woman of Ávila*. Rockport, Mass.: Element Publishing, 1994.

Lincoln, Victoria. *Teresa, a Woman: A Biography of Teresa of Ávila*. Albany, N.Y.: Albany State University Press, 1984.

Medwick, Cathleen. *Teresa of Ávila: The Progress of a Soul*. New York: Image Books, 2001.

St. Teresa of Ávila. *The Interior Castle: Saint Teresa of Ávila*. Translated and edited by E. Allison Peers. New York: Image Books, 1972.

―――. *The Life of Teresa of Jesus: The Autobiography of St. Teresa of Ávila*. Trans. and ed. E. Allison Peers. (Garden City, N.Y.: Image Books, 1950.

Teresa of Ávila. *Vida*, in *The Collected Work*. Washington, D.C.: Institute of Carmelite Studies, 1980.

Recommended Reading

Sojourner Truth

Bernard, Jacqueline. *Journey Toward Freedom: The Story of Sojourner Truth*. New York: Feminist Press, 1990.

Hine, Darlene Clark, ed. *Facts on File Encyclopedia of Black Women in America: The Early Years, 1619–1899*. New York: Facts on File, 1997.

Painter, Nell Irvin. *Sojourner Truth: A Life*. New York: Norton, 1997.

Taylor-Boyd, Susan. *Sojourner Truth: The Courageous Former Slave Whose Eloquence Helped Promote Human Equality*. People Who Have Helped the World Series. Harrisburg, Pa.: Morehouse Publishing Co., 1990.

Truth, Sojourner. *Narrative of Sojourner Truth: A Bondswoman of Olden Time, With a History of Her Labors and Correspondence Drawn from Her "Book of Life."* New York: Oxford University Press, 1991.

Lucretia Mott

Bacon, Margaret Hope. *Valiant Friend*. New York: Walker & Co., 1980.

Mott, Lucretia. *Selected Letters of Lucretia Mott*. Edited by Beverly Wilson Palmer. Urbana: University of Illinois Press, 2002.

Sawyer, Kem Knapp. *Lucretia Mott: Friend of Justice*. Carlisle, Mass.: Discovery Enterprises, 1998.

Steere, Douglas, ed. *Quaker Spirituality: Selected Writings*. Mahwah, N.J.: Paulist Press, 1984.

Dorothy Day

Allaire, James, and Rosemary Broughton. *Praying with Dorothy Day (Companions for the Journey)*. Winona, Minn.: St. Mary's Press, 1995.

Coles, Robert. *Dorothy Day: A Radical Devotion*. Reading, Mass.: Perseus Books, 1987.

Day, Dorothy. *Dorothy Day: Selected Writings*. Edited by Robert Ellsberg. Maryknoll, N.Y.: Orbis Books, 1992.

————. *The Long Loneliness: The Autobiography of Dorothy Day*. San Francisco: HarperCollins, 1997.

Klejment, Anne, and Nancy L. Roberts. *American Catholic Pacifism: The Influence of Dorothy Day and the Catholic Worker Movement*. Westport, Conn.: Praeger, 1996.

Riegle, Rosalie G. *Dorothy Day: Portraits by Those Who Knew Her*. Maryknoll, N.Y.: Orbis Books, 2003.

Recommended Reading

Religion

Allen, Paula Gunn. *The Sacred Hoop*. Boston, Mass.: Beacon Press, 1992.

Anderson, Sherry Ruth. *The Feminine Face of God: The Unfolding of the Sacred in Women*. New York: Bantam Doubleday Dell, 1992.

Birnbaum, Lucia. *Black Madonnas: Feminism, Religion, and Politics in Italy*. Boston: Northeastern University Press, 1993.

CHUNG, Hyun Kyung. *Struggle to Be the Sun Again: Introducing Asian Women's Theology*. Maryknoll, N.Y.: Orbis Books, 1994.

Coogan, Michael D., ed. *The New Oxford Annotated Bible with the Apocrypha*. 3rd ed. New York: Oxford University Press, 2001.

Galland, China. *Longing for Darkness: Tara and the Black Madonna: A Ten-Year Journey*. New York: Viking Penguin, 1991.

Gordon, Anne. *Book of Saints: True Stories of How They Touch Our Lives*. New York: Bantam, 1994.

Isasi-Díaz, Ada María. *En la Lucha (In the Struggle): Elaborating a Mujerista Theology*. 10th Anniversary ed. Minneapolis: Augsburg Fortress, 2003.

Kadel, Andrew. *Matrology: A Bibliography of Writings by Christian Women from the First to the Fifteenth Centuries*. New York: Continuum, 1995.

Norris, Kathleen. *The Cloister Walk*. New York: Riverhead Books, 1997.

Porete, Marguerite. *Mirror of Simple Souls*. Notre Dame, Ind.: University of Notre Dame Press, 1999.

Stanton, Elizabeth Cady. *The Women's Bible*. Amherst, N.Y.: Prometheus Books 1999 [1898].

Thistlethwaite, Susan Brooks, and Mary Potter Engel, eds. *Lift Every Voice: Constructing Christian Theologies from the Underside*. Maryknoll, N.Y.: Orbis, 1998.

townes, emilie, ed. *A Troubling in My Soul: Womanist Perspectives on Evil and Suffering*. Maryknoll, N.Y.: Orbis Books, 1993.

Valentine, Mary. *Saints for Contemporary Women*. Chicago: Thomas More Press, 1987.

Women and History

Barstow, Anne Llewellyn. *Witchcraze: A New History of the European Witch Hunts*. San Francisco: Pandora, 1994.

Bernhard, Virginia, and Elizabeth Fox-Genovese. *The Birth of American Feminism: The Seneca Falls Convention of 1848*. St. James, N.Y.: Brandywine Press, 1995.

Recommended Reading

Braude, Ann. *Radical Spirits: Spiritualism and Women's Rights in Nineteenth-Century America.* Boston: Beacon Press, 1989.

Hatch, Nathan. *Democratization of American Christianity.* New Haven: Yale University Press, 1991.

McGinn, Bernard, ed. *Meister Eckart and the Beguine Mystics: Hadewijch of Brabant, Mechthild of Magdeburg, and Marguerite Porete.* New York: Continuum, 1994.

Murdock, Maureen. *The Heroine's Journey.* Boston: Shambhala Publications, 1990.

Stanton, Elizabeth Cady. *Eighty Years and More (1815–1897): Reminiscences of Elizabeth Cady Stanton.* Boston: Northeastern University Press, 1993 [1898].

————, Susan B. Anthony, and Matilda Joslyn Gage, eds. *The History of Woman Suffrage.* 6 vols. Rochester, N.Y.: Charles Mann, 1889 [1881]–1922.

Steinem, Gloria. "Revaluing Economics," in *Moving Beyond Words: Age, Rage, Sex, Power, Money, Muscles: Breaking Boundaries of Gender.* New York: Simon & Schuster, 1994.

Turning the World Upside Down: The Anti-Slavery Convention of American Women Held in New York City, May 9–12, 1837 [Proceedings]. New York: Feminist Press at City University of New York, 1987 [1837].

Other Writings of Interest

Belenky, Mary Field, et al. *Women's Ways of Knowing: The Development of Self, Voice, and Mind.* New York: Basic Books, 1997.

Carter, Stephen. *The Dissent of the Governed: Law, Religion, and Loyalty.* Cambridge, Mass.: Harvard University Press, 1998.

Ford, Debbie. *The Dark Side of the Light Chasers: Reclaiming Your Power, Creativity, Brilliance, and Dreams.* San Francisco: Berkeley Publishing Group, 2001.

————. *The Secret of the Shadow: The Power of Owning Your Story.* San Francisco: HarperCollins, 2002.

Gilligan, Carol. *In a Different Voice: Psychological Theory and Women's Development.* Cambridge, Mass.: Harvard University Press, 1982.

Goldberger, Nancy Rule, et al., eds. *Knowledge, Difference, and Power: Essays Inspired by Women's Ways of Knowing.* New York: Basic Books, 1996.

Jordan, Judith, et al. *Women's Growth in Connection: Writings from the Stone Center.* New York: Guilford Press, 1991.

Recommended Reading

Jung, Carl Gustav. *Man and His Symbols.* New York: Laurel-Leaf Books, 1968.

————. *The Undiscovered Self.* New York: Back Bay Books, 1972.

Morgan, Robin. *The Anatomy of Freedom: Feminism in Four Dimensions.* New York: Smith Peter, 1995.

O'Reilley, Mary Rose. *Radical Presence: Teaching as Contemplative Practice.* Portsmouth, N.H.: Boynton/Cook Publishers, 1998.

Press, Gerald A., ed. *Plato's Dialogues.* Lanham, Md.: Rowman & Littlefield, 1993.

INDEX

abolitionist feminists, 6–10, 17, 80, 81
    Anti-Slavery Convention of American Women and, 7–8
    backlash against, 8–9
    religion and, 7–8, 8–10, 80
    see also Mott, Lucretia; Truth, Sojourner
abolitionist movement, 7, 76
    Anti-Slavery Convention of American Women and, 7–8
    Mott's role in, 75, 76, 77–78
    Truth's role in, 55–56, 59–61, 62–63
    see also abolitionist feminists
action, 25, 85
    as applied to feminism, 124
    of Mott, 84–85, 103
activism
    of Day, 89–90, 93, 95, 97–98, 98–99
    of Mott, 69–71, 72–73, 74, 75, 76, 77–78, 80–81
    quiet, 82, 83–84, 85
    religion as interconnected with, 5–6, 13–14, 19–21, 72–73, 80, 113, 117
    of St. Teresa, 42
    of Truth, 55–56, 59–61, 61–62, 62–63
    see also abolitionist feminists; abolitionist movement; feminism
Afghanistan, women of, 134

Agros Foundation, 136–37
Aisha, 121
Akron, Ohio, 62
American Anti-Slavery Society (AAS), 76
American Equal Rights Association, 81
Amherst, Mass., 30
Amherst Academy, 31
Anatomy of Freedom, The (Morgan), 17
Andal, 121
Angelou, Maya, 101, 103
Anthony, Susan B., 77, 80, 136
Anti-Slavery Convention of American Women, 7–8, 80
    backlash against, 8–9
    as beginning of feminism, 80
authentic relationships, 96–97, 115
    see also relationships

Battingham, Forster, 91, 92–93
Beguines, xxiv
Beijing conference, 2, 125–26, 130, 140
Beijing Plus Ten, 140
Besant, Annie, xvi
Bett, Mau-Mau, 57
Bhakti movement, 121
Bible, 120
Black Church and Domestic Violence Institute, 126
British Museum, 78
Buber, Martin, 114

Index

Buddhism, and feminism, 121
Bunch, Charlotte, 122

Campbell, Joseph, 23
Carmelite Convent of the
    Incarnation, 45
Carmelite Order of Nuns, 50–51
Carmelites, Discalced, 49, 50
Catherine of Siena, 141
Catholic Church, Catholicism, xxii,
    42–43, 51, 88, 91
    Day's conversion to, 91–93
    Day's influence on, 98–99
    St. Teresa's influence on, 42–43,
        51, 70
    see also Christianity; religion;
        Teresa of Ávila, Saint
Catholic Worker, 95, 98
Catholic Worker movement, xxiv,
    88, 95, 98
Center for Women's Global
    Leadership, 122
Chavez, Cesar, 97
Chesterton, G. K., 127
Child, Lydia Maria, 136
Christianity, xv, xxii, xxv–xxvi, 17,
    73, 140
    Dickinson and, 32
    early years of, 5
    and feminism, 5–6, 9, 13
    Seven Deadly Sins of, 52–53
    shadow aspects and, 52–53
    ultra right of, xvii
    see also Catholic Church,
        Catholicism; religion; Teresa of
        Ávila, Saint
churches:
    house, 120–21
    women's role in, xxiv, 121, 125
    see also religion; *specific religions*
Churchill, Mary, 137
Cloister Walk, The (Norris), 38
Columbia University, 139–40
Communion, 25, 87–88, 113–17
    as applied to feminism, 124
    seeking deeper, 99–100

    see also Day, Dorothy; relation-
        ships
Congress, U.S., 17, 70, 81
connections, see Communion;
    relationships
Constitution, U.S., 81
convents:
    as empowering to women, 45
    St. Teresa's experience in, 44–45
Cousins, Olivia, xxii

Dallas, 105
Dallas Women's Foundation, 110
Dante Alighieri, 52–53
Day, Dorothy, xxiii, xxvi, 22,
    87–100, 104, 141
    activism of, 89–90, 93, 95, 97–98,
        98–99
    background of, 88–90
    Catholic Worker movement and,
        xxiv, 88, 95, 98
    common-law marriage of, 91,
        92–93
    communion work of, 25, 87–88,
        95–97, 98–99, 103
    as considered for sainthood, 22,
        88, 97
    conversion to Catholic Church
        of, 91–93
    death of, 98
    early relationships of, 91
    as "holy woman," 19–21
    influence on Catholic Church of,
        98–99
    jail time of, 90, 97
    as nurse, 90–91
    as pacifist, 97
    religious faith of, 26, 88, 91–93,
        93–94, 95–97, 98–99
    as religious noncomformist,
        94–95
    St. Teresa as inspiration to, 51, 93
    as writer, 89, 90, 91, 92, 93, 98
Day, Tamara Teresa, 51
Declaration of Sentiments and
    Resolutions, 79–80

Index

Depression, Great, 95
Dickinson, Emily, xxiii, xxvi, 22,
    29–39, 85, 104, 141
  background of, 30–31
  death of, 37
  as feminist voice, 31–32, 36
  as "holy woman," 19–21
  introverted nature of, 30–31
  organized religion and, 32
  pain embraced by, 24, 29–30,
    33–36, 38, 103
  physical description of, 32
  poetry of, 29, 31, 32–33, 33–34,
    35–37, 38–39
  published poetry of, 37
  religious faith of, 26, 35, 36–37
  self-imposed isolation of, 33
Discalced Carmelites, 49, 50
Divine Comedy, The, 52–53
domestic violence, 18

early feminism, 5, 6–12, 17, 80, 125
  as funded by men, 135–36
  religious roots of, 10–12, 13, 80,
    128
  Seneca Falls Convention and,
    10–11, 79
  see also abolitionist feminists
Eaton, Kanyere, 113
Ebadi, Shirin, 121
Eleventh Virgin, The (Day), 91
Equal Rights Amendment, 70, 81

"feminine mystique," 105
feminism:
  abolitionist movement and,
    6–10
  backlash against, 8–9, 125
  as beneficial to religion, xxii, xxiii,
    4–5, 13, 16, 18–19, 111,
    122–23, 126–29
  diversity of cultures as beneficial
    to, 126–29, 141–42
  early years of, 5, 6–12, 13, 17–18
  faith-based vs. secular, 1–3,
    12–14

Five Stages Toward Wholeness
  applied to, 123–25
  funding of, 109–13, 135–37
  global vs. local issues in,
    131–34
  healing split between religion
    and, 4–5, 13–14, 14–16, 111,
    117, 122–23, 126–29, 130
  "holy women" in, 19–21, 123
  humility needed in, 133
  incorporating the "we" into,
    137–40
  as interconnected with religion,
    xxi–xxii, xxiii, 5–6, 13–14,
    19–21, 72–73, 80, 113, 128
  listening vs. speaking in, 129,
    130–31
  Native American ties to, 137–38
  relationships as key to strength-
    ening, 137–40
  religious roots of, 10–12, 17, 80,
    125
  second wave of, 5, 17, 17–18
  as secular, xxii, 1–5, 12–16,
    18–19, 110–11, 117
  segmentation in, 132–33
  shadow integration and, 125
  in various religions, 121
  "wholeness" in, 21, 119–20,
    122–26, 129–40
  see also abolitionist feminists; early
    feminism; *specific feminists*
"First Water," 50
Five Stages Toward Wholeness,
  23–27
  as applied to feminism, 123–25
  as universal, xxvii, 101–3
"Fourth Water," 50
"Four Waters of Prayer," 49–50
Freedmen's Hospital, 64
Friedan, Betty, 105

Gage, Matilda Joslyn, 135–36,
  137–38
Galland, China, xxiv–xxv
Gandhi, Mohandas, 128

Index

Garrison, William Lloyd, 72, 74
  Mott's friendship with, 82–83
Gary, Tracy, 109–10
Gathering of Spirited Women,
  140–42
Gilligan, Carol, 66
Goldman, Emma, 26
Great Depression, 95
Grimke, Angelina, 8
Grumm, Christine, 135

Hardenbergh, Isabella, see Truth,
  Sojourner
Hebrew Scriptures, 20
Hendrix, Harville, xxiv, xxviii, 65,
  114–16
Hendrix, Hunter, xxiv, 65, 139–40
Hendrix, Josh, 84
Hendrix, Leah, 39, 98, 132
Hendrix, Mara, 138
Henry de Osso, Saint, 51
Higginson, Thomas, 32, 33, 37
Hildegard of Bingen, xxiv
Hindu saints, 121
History of Woman Suffrage (Stanton),
  80
"holy women," 19–21, 26–27, 67,
  100, 113, 123
  see also specific women
house churches, 120–21
House of Hospitality (Day), 98
Human Rights Watch Women's
  Rights Division, 2
Hunt, Helen LaKelly:
  acceptance of pain by, 105–7
  action taken by, 111–13
  background of, 105–6
  finding of voice by, 109–11
  first marriage of, 106–7
  founding of Sister Fund by, 113
  integration of shadow by, 107–9
  living in Communion and,
    113–17
  pilgrimages of, xxiv–xxv
  relationship struggles of,
    114–15

role in women's funds, 109–10,
  111–12
story of, 105–16
Hunt, H. L., 105–6
Hunt, Jane, 10
Hunt, Ruth Ray, 105–6

I Ching, 37
Imago Relationship Theory,
  xxviii–xxix, 66, 67, 114–15,
  116, 131
  egalitarian partnerships in, 115
Inferno, 53
Inner Truth, hexagram of, 37
Ireland, 74
Islam, xv, xvii, xxv, 121, 134

Jesus, xvi, 12, 20–21, 50, 57, 71, 120
  St. Teresa's vision of, 48
  see also Christianity; religion
Joan of Arc, xxiv, 141
John of the Cross, Saint, xxiii, 50
John, The Gospel According to St.,
  100
Judaism, xv, xvii, xxv–xxvi, 43, 121

Khadija, 121
King, Martin Luther, Jr., 128
King's County Hospital, 90

LaKelly, Kathryn, 83, 107
LaKelly, Kimberly, xxiv, 107,
  136–37
"Let My Joy Be in Lamenting"
  (Teresa of Ávila), 41
Lincoln, Abraham, 64, 65
Lincoln Memorial, 65
Love, Aubra, 126
Luke, The Gospel According to St.,
  39

McClintock, Mary Ann, 10
marriage, egalitarian, 75, 115
Martinson, Pati, 127
matristics, xxiv
Maurin, Peter, 95

Index

Mehta, Sunita, 113, 134
Mendel, Anne, 139
Mirabai, 121
mirroring, 116, 131
    of voice, 66, 99
Mohammed, xvi–xvii, 121
Morgan, Robin, 17, 17–18
Morten, Nelle, 67
Mott, Anna, 75
Mott, James, 73–74, 76, 84
    egalitarian partnership of, 75
    pacifism of, 81–82
    reform work of, 74–75
Mott, Lucretia, xxiii, xxvi, 10,
        20–21, 22, 61, 69–85, 104,
        141
    as abolitionist activist, 44, 75, 76,
        77–78
    acknowledged as minister, 73
    action taken by, 25, 84–85, 103
    appreciation of Native American
        cultures by, 137–38
    background of, 69, 70–71
    Declaration of Sentiments and
        Resolutions and, 79–80
    egalitarian partnership of, 75
    Equal Rights Amendment named
        after, 69–70, 81
    Garrison's friendship with, 82–83
    as "holy woman," 19–21
    marriage of, 73–75
    pacifism of, 81–82
    physical appearance of, 72
    as president of American Equal
        Rights Association, 81
    quiet activism of, 82, 83–84, 85
    religious faith of, 26, 69, 70–71,
        72–73, 76, 81, 84–85
    Stanton's alliance with, 77–79,
        80–81
    as women's rights activist, 69–71,
        72–73, 74, 80–81
Mount Holyoke Female Seminary,
        31
Ms. Foundation for Women, 110
Muslim feminists, 121, 134

Nantucket Island, Mass., 70–71
Narrative of Sojourner Truth, The, 55
National Anti-Slavery Conventions
    of American Women, 76
National Organization for
    Women, 5
National Women's Hall of Fame,
    xxiii
Native Americans, xxv
    feminist ties to, 137–38
New Masses, 90
New Testament, 94, 140
New York Call, 90
New York Women's Foundation,
    13–14, 112, 135, 139
Norris, Kathleen, 38

On Pilgrimage: The Sixties (Day), 98
O'Reilley, Mary, 22

pain, 24, 29–30, 65
    as agent for transformation,
        38–39, 105–7
    as applied to feminism, 123
    see also Dickinson, Emily
Paradise, 52
patristics, xxiv
Paul, Saint, 120
Pax Christi, 97
Pert, Florence, 14
Philadelphia Female Anti-Slavery
    Society, 76
philanthropy, women's, see women's
    funds
Phoebe, 120
Productive Outreach for Women,
    140
Project People Foundation, 132
Psalm 85, 98
Purgatory, 52

Quakers, 6–7, 69, 70, 73, 74, 81
    egalitarian philosophy of, 71, 75
    of Nantucket, 71
    see also Mott, Lucretia; religion
    quiet activism, 82, 83–84, 85

Index

Randy (author's first husband), 106, 107

relationships, xix, 113–14
  and achieving "wholeness," 25–26, 116
  authentic, 96–97, 115
  Buber's theory on, 114
  Hunt's struggles with, 114–15, 115–16
  importance of equality in, 114–16
  incorporating the "we" into, 137–38, 139
  as key to feminist movement, 137–40
  see also Communion

religion:
  in abolitionist feminism, 7–8, 8–10, 80
  as beneficial to feminism, xxii, xxiii, 4–5, 13, 16, 18–19, 111, 122–23, 126–29
  in early feminism, 10–12, 13, 80
  feminist split from, xxii, 1–5, 12–16, 18–19, 110–11, 117
  healing the split between feminism and, 4–5, 13–14, 14–16, 18–19, 111, 117, 122–23, 126–29, 130
  "holy women" and, 19–21
  as interconnected with feminism, xxi–xxii, xxiii, 5–6, 13–14, 19–21, 72–73, 80, 113, 128
  rise of the feminine in, xvii, 120–21
  and seeking Communion, 99–100
  wholeness of, 119–21
  women's oppression in, 3–5, 13–14, 79, 110–11, 121, 125
  women's role in, 120–21
  see also feminism; specific religions

RisingLeaf Watershed Arts, 138
Roman Catholic Church, see Catholic Church, Catholicism

Sammon, Jane, 98
"Second Water," 50

second wave of feminism, 5, 17, 17–18
Seder, xvii
Seneca Falls, N.Y., 10, 79
Seneca Falls Convention, 10–11, 79, 113, 137
Seneca Falls Declaration of Sentiments and Resolutions, 10
Seneca Indians, 137
Seven Deadly Sins, 52–53
shadow, 24, 41–42, 46, 65
  as applied to feminism, 123–24, 125, 126–29
  integration of, 51–53, 107–9, 126–29
  see also Teresa de Ávila, Saint
Silver Lake, Ind., 62
Sister Fund, 113, 127, 131, 134
slaves, slavery, 17
  Quakers opposition to, 71
  see also abolitionist feminists; Truth, Sojourner
Socialist Party, 89
Society of Friends, see Quakers 73
South Africa, 132
Spain, golden age of, 43
  Catholicism in, 45
  women's role in, 45
Spanish Inquisition, 49
Stanton, Elizabeth Cady, 10, 75, 120, 121, 136
  Declaration of Sentiments and Resolutions and, 79–80
  Mott's alliance with, 77–79, 80–81
Stein, Edith, 51
Steinem, Gloria, 108, 119, 139
  introduction by, xv–xix
Stone, Lucy, 61
Stone Center at Wellesley, 15
stories, sharing of, xxvii–xxviii, 101–4
"Sunday School Circa 1950" (Walker), xviii

Index

Taliban, 134
Tarry-Chard, Linda, 131–32
Teamsters Union (IBT), 97
Teresa of Ávila, Saint, xxiii, xxiv,
    xxvi, 22, 41–53, 104, 141
  activism of, 42
  adolescent rebellion of, 43–44,
    44–45
  background of, 41–42, 43–44
  canonization of, 42, 43
  Carmelite order entered into by,
    45–46
  church denouncing of, 49
  conversion experience of, 48–49
  death of, 50
  as Doctor of the Church, 42–43
  first convent of, 44–45
  "Four Waters of Prayer" by, 49–50
  as "holy woman," 19–21
  integration of shadow self by, 24,
    41–42, 47–48, 48–49, 51–52,
    103, 126
  new order founded by, 49, 50
  religious faith of, 26, 42, 43, 44,
    47–48, 51
  spiritual conflicts of, 45–47
  surviving influence of, 50–51
Teresian Order, 51
Theosophy, xvi, xix
"There is a pain so utter"
    (Dickinson), 29
"Third Water," 50
Thomas, Dorothy Q., 1, 2
"Truth of God . . . The Right-
    eousness of God" (Mott), 69
Truth, Sojourner, xxiii, xxvi, 22,
    55–67, 72, 104, 141
  as abolitionist activist, 55–56,
    59–61, 62–63
  Akron speech of, 62
  background of, 56–57
  changing of name by, 58–59
  death of, 64
  as delegate to Women's Rights
    Convention, 61
  detractors of, 62–63

escape from slavery of, 58
finding of voice by, 24, 55–56,
    59–61, 64–65, 103, 130
  as "holy woman," 19–21
  Lincoln's respect for, 64, 65
  as public speaker, 56, 59–61, 62,
    63–64
  religious faith of, 26, 57–58,
    63–64, 65
  as slave, 55, 55–56, 57, 61, 62, 64
  spiritual pilgrimage of, 58–59,
    64–65
  as women's rights activist, 55–56,
    61–62
Tsomo, Karma Lekshe, 121
Tubman, Harriet, 128, 141

Underground Railroad, 74
Union Theological Seminary, xxiv
United Farm Workers of America,
    97
United Nations Fourth World
    Conference on Women, 2,
    125–26, 130, 140

Vatican II, 97
Virgin Mary, 43
voice, 24, 55–56
  as applied to feminism, 124
  finding of, 65–67
  inner vs. outer, 66, 67, 107
  mirroring of, 66, 99
  see also Truth, Sojourner

Walker, Alice, xviii
wealth, as power, 106
"wholeness," xxi–xxii, 99–100, 105,
    117
  in feminism, 21, 111, 119–20,
    122–26, 129–40
  five stages toward, 23–27, 101–3
  listening vs. speaking in
    achieving, 66–67, 129,
    130–31
  relationships as key to achieving,
    116

Index

"wholeness" (*cont.*)
  of religion, 119–21
  as universal journey, 101–3,
    103–4
  see also specific stages
Willis, Janice Dean, 121
Wilson, Marie, 111
women:
  convents as empowering to, 45
  Five Stages Toward Wholeness as
    universal to, 101–3
  "holy," 19–21, 26–27, 67, 100
  inner journey of, 23–27
  oppression of, in religion, 3–5,
    13–14, 79, 110–11, 121, 125
  role in churches of, xxiv, 121, 125
  see also feminism; *specific women*
Women for Afghan Women, 134

Women's Bible (Stanton, ed.), 120
Women's Foundation of San
  Francisco, 109
Women's Funding Network, 14, 135
women's funds, 109–13, 135–37
  early feminism and, 135–36
  growth of, 112, 113, 136
women's movement, *see* feminism
Women's Rights Convention (1850),
  61
Women's Rights Convention
  (Seneca Falls), 10–11, 79, 113,
  137
Woolf, Virginia, 103
World Anti-Slavery Meeting, 76
Wright, Martha, 10

Yahweh, 55

Made in the USA
Las Vegas, NV
04 February 2024